Night

Elie Wiesel

••••

With
Connected Readings

PRENTICE HALL
Upper Saddle River, New Jersey
Needham, Massachusetts
Glenview, Illinois

ISBN 0-13-437494-0

1 2 3 4 5 6 7 8 9 10   03 02 01 00 99

PRENTICE HALL

Acknowledgments

Grateful acknowledgment is made to the following for permission to reprint copyrighted material:

Georges Borchardt, Inc.
"Bitburg" by Elie Wiesel from *The Kingdom of Memory*. Copyright © 1990 by Elirion Associates, Inc. Reprinted by permission of Georges Borchardt, Inc.

Doubleday, a division of Random House, Inc.
From *Anne Frank: The Diary of a Young Girl* by Anne Frank. Copyright 1952 by Otto H. Frank. Used by permission of Doubleday, a division of Random House, Inc.

Harcourt Inc.
Excerpts from *Anne Frank: A Portrait in Courage* by Ernest Schnabel, English translation by Richard and Clara Winston. Copyright © 1958 by Otto H. Frank and renewed 1986 by Justina Winston Gregory and Krishna Winston. Reprinted by permission of the publisher, Harcourt, Inc.

Hill and Wang, a division of Farrar, Straus & Giroux, Inc.
Night by Elie Wiesel. Copyright © 1960 by MacGibbon and Kee. Copyright renewed © 1988 by The Collins Publishing Group. All rights reserved. Published by arrangement with Hill and Wang, a division of Farrar, Straus & Giroux, Inc.

Lucent Books, Inc.
"The Warsaw Ghetto Uprising" from *The Resistance* by Deborah Bachrach. Copyright 1998 by Lucent Books, Inc. Reprinted with permission of Lucent Books, Inc.

Newsweek, Inc.
"We Are Witnesses" by Kenneth L. Woodward from *Newsweek*, 4/26/93, © 1993 Newsweek, Inc. All rights reserved. Reprinted by permission.

(Acknowledgments continue on p. 158.)

Contents

Night

Night

Elie Wiesel

1

THEY called him Moshe the Beadle, as though he had never had a surname in his life. He was a man of all work at a Hasidic synagogue. The Jews of Sighet—that little town in Transylvania where I spent my childhood—were very fond of him. He was very poor and lived humbly. Generally my fellow townspeople, though they would help the poor, were not particularly fond of them. Moshe the Beadle was the exception. Nobody ever felt embarrassed by him. Nobody ever felt encumbered by his presence. He was a past master in the art of making himself insignificant, of seeming invisible.

Physically he was as awkward as a clown. He made people smile, with his waiflike timidity. I loved his great, dreaming eyes, their gaze lost in the distance. He spoke little. He used to sing, or, rather, to chant. Such snatches as you could hear told of the suffering of the divinity, of the Exile of Providence, who, according to the cabbala, awaits his deliverance in that of man.

I got to know him toward the end of 1941. I was twelve. I believed profoundly. During the day I studied the Talmud, and at night I ran to the synagogue to weep over the destruction of the Temple.

One day I asked my father to find me a master to guide me in my studies of the cabbala.

"You're too young for that. Maimonides said it was only at thirty that one had the right to venture into the perilous world of mysticism. You must first study the basic subjects within your own understanding."

My father was a cultured, rather unsentimental man. There was never any display of emotion, even at home. He was more concerned with others than with his own family. The Jewish community in Sighet held him in the greatest esteem. They often used to consult him about public matters and even about private ones. There were four of us children: Hilda, the eldest; then Béa; I was the third, and the only son; the baby of the family was Tzipora.

My parents ran a shop. Hilda and Béa helped them with the work. As for me, they said my place was at school.

"There aren't any cabbalists at Sighet," my father would repeat.

He wanted to drive the notion out of my head. But it was in vain. I found a master for myself, Moshe the Beadle.

He had noticed me one day at dusk, when I was praying.

"Why do you weep when you pray?" he asked me, as though he had known me a long time.

"I don't know why," I answered, greatly disturbed.

The question had never entered my head. I wept because—because of something inside me that felt the need for tears. That was all I knew.

"Why do you pray?" he asked me, after a moment.

Why did I pray? A strange question. Why did I live? Why did I breathe?

"I don't know why," I said, even more disturbed and ill at ease. "I don't know why."

After that day I saw him often. He explained to me with great insistence that every question possessed a power that did not lie in the answer.

"Man raises himself toward God by the questions he asks Him," he was fond of repeating. "That is the true dialogue. Man questions God and God answers. But we don't understand His answers. We can't understand them. Because they come from the depths of the soul, and they stay there until death. You will find the true answers, Eliezer, only within yourself!"

"And why do you pray, Moshe?" I asked him.

"I pray to the God within me that He will give me the strength to ask Him the right questions."

We talked like this nearly every evening. We used to stay in the synagogue after all the faithful had left, sitting in the gloom, where a few half-burned candles still gave a flickering light.

One evening I told him how unhappy I was because I could not find a master in Sighet to instruct me in the Zohar, the cabbalistic books, the secrets of Jewish mysticism. He smiled indulgently. After a long silence, he said:

"There are a thousand and one gates leading into the orchard of mystical truth. Every human being has his own gate. We must never make the mistake of wanting to enter the orchard by any gate but our own. To do this is dangerous for the one who enters and also for those who are already there."

And Moshe the Beadle, the poor barefoot of Sighet, talked to me for long hours of the revelations and mysteries of the cabbala. It was with him that my initiation began. We would read together, ten times over, the same page of the Zohar. Not to learn it by heart, but to extract the divine essence from it.

And throughout those evenings a conviction grew in me that Moshe the Beadle would draw me with him into eternity, into that time where question and answer would become *one*.

Then one day they expelled all the foreign Jews from Sighet. And Moshe the Beadle was a foreigner.

Crammed into cattle trains by Hungarian police, they wept bitterly. We stood on the platform and wept too. The train disappeared on the horizon; it left nothing behind but its thick, dirty smoke.

I heard a Jew behind me heave a sigh.

"What can we expect?" he said. "It's war. . . ."

The deportees were soon forgotten. A few days after they had gone, people were saying that they had arrived in Galicia, were working there, and were even satisfied with their lot.

Several days passed. Several weeks. Several months. Life had returned to normal. A wind of calmness and reassurance blew through our houses. The traders were doing good business, the students lived buried in their books, and the children played in the streets.

One day, as I was just going into the synagogue, I saw, sitting on a bench near the door, Moshe the Beadle.

He told his story and that of his companions. The train full of deportees had crossed the Hungarian frontier and on Polish territory had been taken in charge by the Gestapo. There it had stopped. The Jews had to get out and climb into lorries. The lorries drove toward a forest. The Jews were made to get out. They were made to dig huge graves. And when they had finished their work, the Gestapo began theirs. Without passion, without haste, they slaughtered their prisoners. Each one had to go up to the hole and present his neck. Babies were thrown into the air and the machine gunners used them as targets. This was in the forest of Galicia, near Kolomaye. How had Moshe the Beadle escaped? Miraculously. He was wounded in the leg and taken for dead. . . .

Through long days and nights, he went from one Jewish house to another, telling the story of Malka, the young girl who had taken three days to die, and of Tobias, the tailor, who had begged to be killed before his sons. . . .

Moshe had changed. There was no longer any joy in his eyes. He no longer sang. He no longer talked to me of God or of the cabbala, but only of what he had seen. People refused not only to believe his stories, but even to listen to them.

"He's just trying to make us pity him. What an imagination he has!" they said. Or even: "Poor fellow. He's gone mad."

And as for Moshe, he wept.

"Jews, listen to me. It's all I ask of you. I don't want money or pity. Only listen to me," he would cry between prayers at dusk and the evening prayers.

I did not believe him myself. I would often sit with him in the evening after the service, listening to his stories and trying my hardest to understand his grief. I felt only pity for him.

"They take me for a madman," he would whisper, and tears, like drops of wax, flowed from his eyes.

Once, I asked him this question:

"Why are you so anxious that people should believe what you say? In your place, I shouldn't care whether they believed me or not. . . ."

He closed his eyes, as though to escape time.

"You don't understand," he said in despair. "You can't understand. I have been saved miraculously. I managed to get back here. Where did I get the strength from? I wanted to come back to Sighet to tell you the story of my death. So that you could prepare yourselves while there was still time. To live? I don't attach any importance to my life any more. I'm alone. No, I wanted to come back, and to warn you. And see how it is, no one will listen to me. . . ."

That was toward the end of 1942. Afterward life returned to normal. The London radio, which we listened to every evening, gave us heartening news: the daily bombardment of Germany; Stalingrad; preparation for the second front. And we, the Jews of Sighet, were waiting for better days, which would not be long in coming now.

I continued to devote myself to my studies. By day, the Talmud, at night, the cabbala. My father was occupied with his business and the doings of the community. My grandfather had come to celebrate the New Year with us, so that he could attend the services of the famous rabbi of Borsche. My mother began to think that it was high time to find a suitable young man for Hilda.

Thus the year 1943 passed by.

Spring 1944. Good news from the Russian front. No doubt could remain now of Germany's defeat. It was only a question of time—of months or weeks perhaps.

The trees were in blossom. This was a year like any other, with its springtime, its betrothals, its weddings and births.

People said: "The Russian army's making gigantic strides forward . . . Hitler won't be able to do us any harm, even if he wants to."

Yes, we even doubted that he wanted to exterminate us.

Was he going to wipe out a whole people? Could he exterminate a population scattered throughout so many countries? So many millions! What methods could he use? And in the middle of the twentieth century!

Besides, people were interested in everything—in strategy, in diplomacy, in politics, in Zionism—but not in their own fate.

Even Moshe the Beadle was silent. He was weary of speaking. He wandered in the synagogue or in the streets, with his eyes down, his back bent, avoiding people's eyes.

At that time, it was still possible to obtain emigration permits for Palestine. I had asked my father to sell out, liquidate his business, and leave.

"I'm too old, my son," he replied. "I'm too old to start a new life. I'm too old to start from scratch again in a country so far away. . . ."

The Budapest radio announced that the Fascist party had come into power. Horthy had been forced to ask one of the leaders of the Nyilas party to form a new government.

Still this was not enough to worry us. Of course we had heard about the Fascists, but they were still just an abstraction to us. This was only a change in the administration.

The following day, there was more disturbing news: with government permission, German troops had entered Hungarian territory.

Here and there, anxiety was aroused. One of our friends, Berkovitz, who had just returned from the capital, told us:

"The Jews in Budapest are living in an atmosphere of fear and terror. There are anti-Semitic incidents every day, in the streets, in the trains. The Fascists are attacking Jewish shops and synagogues. The situation is getting very serious."

This news spread like wildfire through Sighet. Soon it was on everyone's lips. But not for long. Optimism soon revived.

"The Germans won't get as far as this. They'll stay in Budapest. There are strategic and political reasons. . . ."

Before three days had passed, German army cars had appeared in our streets.

Anguish. German soldiers—with their steel helmets, and their emblem, the death's head.

However, our first impressions of the Germans were most reassuring. The officers were billeted in private houses, even in the homes of Jews. Their attitude toward their hosts was distant, but polite. They never demanded the impossible, made no unpleasant comments, and even smiled occasionally at the mistress of the house. One German officer lived in the house opposite ours. He had a room with the Kahn family. They said he was a charming man—calm, likable, polite, and sympathetic. Three days after he moved in he brought Madame Kahn a box of chocolates. The optimists rejoiced.

"Well, there you are, you see! What did we tell you? You wouldn't believe us. There they are *your* Germans! What do you think of them? Where is their famous cruelty?"

The Germans were already in the town, the Fascists were already in power, the verdict had already been pronounced, yet the Jews of Sighet continued to smile.

The week of Passover. The weather was wonderful. My mother bustled round her kitchen. There were no longer any synagogues open. We gathered in private houses: the Germans were not to be provoked. Practically every rabbi's flat became a house of prayer.

We drank, we ate, we sang. The Bible bade us rejoice during the seven days of the feast, to be happy. But our hearts were not in it. Our hearts had been beating more rapidly for some days. We wished the feast were over, so that we should not have to play this comedy any longer.

On the seventh day of Passover the curtain rose. The Germans arrested the leaders of the Jewish community.

From that moment, everything happened very quickly. The race toward death had begun.

The first step: Jews would not be allowed to leave their houses for three days—on pain of death.

Moshe the Beadle came running to our house.

"I warned you," he cried to my father. And, without waiting for a reply, he fled.

That same day the Hungarian police burst into all the Jewish houses in the street. A Jew no longer had the right to keep in his house gold, jewels, or any objects of value. Everything had to be handed over to the authorities—on pain of death. My father went down into the cellar and buried our savings.

At home, my mother continued to busy herself with her usual tasks. At times she would pause and gaze at us, silent.

When the three days were up, there was a new decree: every Jew must wear the yellow star.

Some of the prominent members of the community came to see my father—who had highly placed connections in the Hungarian police—to ask him what he thought of the situation. My father did not consider it so grim—but perhaps he did not want to dishearten the others or rub salt in their wounds:

"The yellow star? Oh well, what of it? You don't die of it. . . ."

(Poor Father! Of what then did you die?)

But already they were issuing new decrees. We were no longer allowed to go into restaurants or cafés, to travel on the railway, to attend the synagogue, to go out into the street after six o'clock.

Then came the ghetto.

Two ghettos were set up in Sighet. A large one, in the center of the town, occupied four streets, and another smaller one extended over several small side streets in the outlying district. The street where we lived, Serpent Street, was inside the first ghetto. We still lived, therefore, in our own house. But as it was at the corner, the windows facing the outside street had to be blocked up. We gave up some of our rooms to relatives who had been driven out of their flats.

Little by little life returned to normal. The barbed wire which fenced us in did not cause us any real fear. We even thought ourselves rather well off; we were entirely self-contained. A little Jewish republic. . . . We appointed a Jewish Council, a Jewish police, an office for social assistance, a labor committee, a hygiene department—a whole government machinery.

Everyone marveled at it. We should no longer have before our eyes those hostile faces, those hate-laden stares. Our fear and anguish were at an end. We were living among Jews, among brothers. . . .

Of course, there were still some unpleasant moments. Every day the Germans came to fetch men to stoke coal on the military trains. There were not many volunteers for work of this kind. But apart from that the atmosphere was peaceful and reassuring.

The general opinion was that we were going to remain in the ghetto until the end of the war, until the arrival of the Red Army. Then everything would be as before. It was neither German nor Jew who ruled the ghetto—it was illusion.

On the Saturday before Pentecost, in the spring sunshine, people strolled, carefree and unheeding, through the swarming streets. They chatted happily. The children played games on the pavements. With some of my schoolmates, I sat in the Ezra Malik gardens, studying a treatise on the Talmud.

Night fell. There were twenty people gathered in our back yard. My father was telling them anecdotes and expounding his own views on the situation. He was a good story teller.

Suddenly the gate opened and Stern—a former tradesman who had become a policeman—came in and took my father aside. Despite the gathering dusk, I saw my father turn pale.

"What's the matter?" we all asked him.

"I don't know. I've been summoned to an extraordinary meeting of the council. Something must have happened."

The good story he had been in the middle of telling us was to remain unfinished.

"I'm going there," he went on. "I shall be back as soon as I can. I'll tell you all about it. Wait for me."

We were prepared to wait for some hours. The back yard became like the hall outside an operating room. We were only waiting for the door to open—to see the opening of the firmament itself. Other neighbors, having heard rumors, had come to join us. People looked at their watches. The time passed very slowly. What could such a long meeting mean?

"I've got a premonition of evil," said my mother. "This afternoon I noticed some new faces in the ghetto—two German officers, from the Gestapo, I believe. Since we've been here, not a single officer has ever shown himself. . . ."

It was nearly midnight. No one had wanted to go to bed. A few people had paid a flying visit to their homes to see that everything was all right. Others had returned home, but they left instructions that they were to be told as soon as my father came back.

At last the door opened and he appeared. He was pale. At once he was surrounded.

"What happened? Tell us what happened! Say something!"

How avid we were at that moment for one word of confidence, one sentence to say that there were no grounds for fear, that the meeting could not have been more commonplace, more routine, that it had only been a question of social welfare, of sanitary arrangements! But one glance at my father's haggard face was enough.

"I have terrible news," he said at last. "Deportation."

The ghetto was to be completely wiped out. We were to leave street by street, starting the following day.

We wanted to know everything, all the details. The news had stunned everyone, yet we wanted to drain the bitter draft to the dregs.

"Where are we being taken?"

This was a secret. A secret from all except one: the President of the Jewish Council. But he would not say; he *could* not say. The Gestapo had threatened to shoot him if he talked.

"There are rumors going around," said my father in a broken voice, "that we're going somewhere in Hungary, to work in the brick factories. Apparently, the reason is that the front is too close here. . . ."

And, after a moment's silence, he added:

"Each person will be allowed to take only his own personal belongings. A bag on our backs, some food, a few clothes. Nothing else."

Again a heavy silence.

"Go and wake the neighbors up," said my father. "So that they can get ready."

The shadows beside me awoke as from a long sleep. They fled, silently, in all directions.

For a moment we were alone. Then suddenly Batia Reich, a relative who was living with us, came into the room:

"There's someone knocking on the blocked-up window, the one that faces outside!"

It was not until after the war that I learned who it was that had knocked. It was an inspector in the Hungarian police, a friend of my father. Before we went into the ghetto, he had said to us: "Don't worry. If you're in any danger, I'll warn you." If he could have spoken to us that evening, we could perhaps have fled. . . . But by the time we had managed to open the window, it was too late. There was no one outside.

The ghetto awoke. One by one, lights came on in the windows.

I went into the house of one of my father's friends. I woke up the head of the household, an old man with a gray beard and the eyes of a dreamer. He was stooped from long nights of study.

"Get up, sir, get up! You've got to get ready for the journey! You're going to be expelled from here tomorrow with your whole family, and all the rest of the Jews. Where to? Don't ask me, sir. Don't ask me any questions. Only God could answer you. For heaven's sake, get up."

He had not understood a word of what I was saying. He probably thought I had gone out of my mind.

"What tale is this? Get ready for the journey? What journey? Why? What's going on? Have you gone mad?"

Still half asleep, he stared at me with terror-stricken eyes, as though he expected me to burst out laughing and say in the end, "Get back to bed. Go to sleep. Pleasant dreams. Nothing's happened at all. It was just a joke."

My throat was dry, the words choked in it, paralyzing my lips. I could not say any more.

Then he understood. He got out of bed and with automatic movements began to get dressed. Then he went up to the bed where his wife slept and touched her brow with infinite tenderness; she opened her eyes, and it seemed to me that her lips were brushed by a smile. Then he went to his children's beds and woke them swiftly, dragging them from their dreams. I fled.

Time passed very quickly. It was already four o'clock in the morning. My father ran to right and left, exhausted, comforting friends, running to the Jewish Council to see if the edict had not been revoked in the meantime. To the very last moment, a germ of hope stayed alive in our hearts.

The women were cooking eggs, roasting meat, baking cakes, and making knapsacks. The children wandered all over the place, hanging their heads, not knowing what to do with themselves, where to go, to keep from getting in the way of the grown-ups. Our back yard had become a real market place. Household treasures, valuable carpets, silver candelabra, prayer books, Bibles, and other religious articles littered the dusty ground beneath a wonderfully blue sky; pathetic objects which looked as though they had never belonged to anyone.

By eight o'clock in the morning, a weariness like molten lead began to settle in the veins, the limbs, the brain. I was in the midst of my prayers when suddenly there were shouts in the street. I tore myself from my phylacteries and ran to the window. Hungarian police had entered the ghetto and were shouting in the neighboring street:

"All Jews outside! Hurry!"

Some Jewish police went into the houses, saying in broken voices:

"The time's come now . . . you've got to leave all this. . . ."

The Hungarian police struck out with truncheons and rifle butts, to right and left, without reason, indiscriminately, their blows falling upon old men and women, children and invalids alike.

One by one the houses emptied, and the street filled with people and bundles. By ten o'clock, all the condemned were outside.

The police took a roll call, once, twice, twenty times. The heat was intense. Sweat streamed from faces and bodies.

Children cried for water.

Water? There was plenty, close at hand, in the houses, in the yards, but they were forbidden to break the ranks.

"Water! Mummy! Water!"

The Jewish police from the ghetto were able to go and fill a few jugs secretly. Since my sisters and I were destined for the last convoy and we were still allowed to move about, we helped them as well as we could.

Then, at last, at one o'clock in the afternoon, came the signal to leave.

There was joy—yes, joy. Perhaps they thought that God could have devised no torment in hell worse than that of sitting there among the bundles, in the middle of the road, beneath a blazing sun; that anything would be preferable to that. They began their journey without a backward glance at the abandoned streets, the dead, empty houses, the gardens, the tombstones. . . . On everyone's back was a pack. In everyone's eyes was suffering drowned in tears. Slowly, heavily, the procession made its way to the gate of the ghetto.

And there was I, on the pavement, unable to make a move. Here came the Rabbi, his back bent, his face shaved, his pack on his back. His mere presence among the deportees added a touch of unreality to the scene. It was like a page torn from some story book, from some historical novel about the captivity of Babylon or the Spanish Inquisition.

One by one they passed in front of me, teachers, friends, others, all those I had been afraid of, all those I once could have laughed at, all those I had lived with over the years. They went by, fallen, dragging their packs, dragging their lives, deserting their homes, the years of their childhood, cringing like beaten dogs.

They passed without a glance in my direction. They must have envied me.

The procession disappeared round the corner of the street. A few paces farther on, and they would have passed beyond the ghetto walls.

The street was like a market place that had suddenly been abandoned. Everything could be found there: suitcases, portfolios, briefcases, knives, plates, banknotes, papers, faded portraits. All those things that people had thought of taking with them, and which in the end they had left behind. They had lost all value.

Everywhere rooms lay open. Doors and windows gaped onto the emptiness. Everything was free for anyone, belonging to nobody. It was simply a matter of helping oneself. An open tomb.

A hot summer sun.

We had spent the day fasting. But we were not very hungry. We were exhausted.

My father had accompanied the deportees as far as the entrance of the ghetto. They first had to go through the big synagogue, where they were minutely searched, to see that they were not taking away any gold, silver, or other objects of value. There were outbreaks of hysteria and blows with the truncheons.

"When is our turn coming?" I asked my father.

"The day after tomorrow. At least—at least, unless things turn out differently. A miracle, perhaps. . . ."

Where were the people being taken to? Didn't anyone know yet? No, the secret was well kept.

Night had fallen. That evening we went to bed early. My father said:

"Sleep well, children. It's not until the day after tomorrow, Tuesday."

Monday passed like a small summer cloud, like a dream in the first daylight hours.

Busy with getting our packs ready, with baking bread and cakes, we no longer thought of anything. The verdict had been delivered.

That evening, our mother made us go to bed very early, to conserve our strength, she said. It was our last night at home.

I was up at dawn. I wanted time to pray before we were expelled.

My father had got up earlier to go and seek information. He came back at about eight o'clock. Good news: it wasn't today that we were leaving the town. We were only to move into the little ghetto. There we would wait for the last transport. We should be the last to leave.

At nine o'clock, Sunday's scenes began all over again. Policemen with truncheons yelling:

"All Jews outside!"

We were ready. I was the first to leave. I did not want to see my parents' faces. I did not want to break into tears. We stayed sitting down in the middle of the road, as the others had done the day before yesterday. There was the same infernal heat. The same thirst. But there was no longer anyone left to bring us water.

I looked at our house, where I had spent so many years in my search for God; in fasting in order to hasten the coming of the Messiah; in imagining what my life would be like. Yet I felt little sorrow. I thought of nothing.

"Get up! Count off!"

Standing. Counting off. Sitting down. Standing up again. On the ground once more. Endlessly. We waited impatiently to be fetched. What were they waiting for? At last the order came:

"Forward march!"

My father wept. It was the first time I had ever seen him weep. I had never imagined that he could. As for my mother, she walked with a set expression on her face, without a word, deep in thought. I looked at my little sister Tzipora, her fair hair well combed, a red coat over her arm, a little girl of seven. The bundle on her back was too heavy for her. She gritted her teeth. She knew by now that it would be useless to complain. The police were striking out with their truncheons. "Faster!" I had no strength left. The journey had only just begun, and I felt so weak. . . .

"Faster! Faster! Get on with you, lazy swine!" yelled the Hungarian police.

It was from that moment that I began to hate them, and my hate is still the only link between us today. They were our first oppressors. They were the first of the faces of hell and death.

We were ordered to run. We advanced in double time. Who would have thought we were so strong? Behind their windows, behind their shutters, our compatriots looked out at us as we passed.

At last we reached our destination. Throwing our bags to the ground, we sank down:

"Oh God, Lord of the Universe, take pity upon us in Thy great mercy. . . ."

The little ghetto. Three days before, people had still been living there—the people who owned the things we were using now. They had been expelled. Already we had completely forgotten them.

The disorder was greater than in the big ghetto. The people must have been driven out unexpectedly. I went to see the rooms where my uncle's family had lived. On the table there was a half-finished bowl of soup. There was a pie waiting to be put in the oven. Books were littered about on the floor. Perhaps my uncle had had dreams of taking them with him?

We settled in. (What a word!) I went to get some wood; my sisters lit the fire. Despite her own weariness, my mother began to prepare a meal.

"We must keep going, we must keep going," she kept on repeating.

The people's morale was not too bad; we were beginning to get used to the situation. In the street, they even went so far as to have optimistic conversations. The Boche would not have time to expel us, they were saying . . . as far as those who had already been deported were concerned, it was too bad; no more could be done. But they would probably allow us to live out our wretched little lives here, until the end of the war.

The ghetto was not guarded. Everyone could come and go as they pleased. Our old servant, Martha, came to see us. Weeping bitterly, she begged us to come to her village, where she could give us a safe refuge. My father did not want to hear of it.

"You can go if you want to," he said to me and to my older sisters. "I shall stay here with your mother and the child. . . ."

Naturally, we refused to be separated.

Night. No one prayed, so that the night would pass quickly. The stars were only sparks of the fire which devoured us. Should that fire die out one day, there would be nothing left in the sky but dead stars, dead eyes.

There was nothing else to do but to get into bed, into the beds of the absent ones; to rest, to gather one's strength.

At dawn, there was nothing left of this melancholy. We felt as though we were on holiday. People were saying:

"Who knows? Perhaps we are being deported for our own good. The front isn't very far off; we shall soon be able to hear the guns. And then the civilian population would be evacuated anyway. . . ."

"Perhaps they were afraid we might help the guerrillas. . . ."

"If you ask me, the whole business of deportation is just a farce. Oh yes, don't laugh. The Boches just want to steal our jewelry. They know we've buried everything, and that they'll have to hunt for it: it's easier when the owners are on holiday. . . ."

On holiday!

These optimistic speeches, which no one believed, helped to pass the time. The few days we lived here went by pleasantly enough, in peace. People were better disposed toward one another. There were no longer any questions of wealth, of social

distinction, and importance, only people all condemned to the
same fate—still unknown.

Saturday, the day of rest, was chosen for our expulsion.

The night before, we had the traditional Friday evening meal.
We said the customary grace for the bread and wine and swallowed our food without a word. We were, we felt, gathered for
the last time round the family table. I spent the night turning
over thoughts and memories in my mind, unable to find sleep.

At dawn, we were in the street, ready to leave. This time
there were no Hungarian police. An agreement had been made
with the Jewish Council that they should organize it all themselves.

Our convoy went toward the main synagogue. The town
seemed deserted. Yet our friends of yesterday were probably
waiting behind their shutters for the moment when they could
pillage our houses.

The synagogue was like a huge station: luggage and tears.
The altar was broken, the hangings torn down, the walls bare.
There were so many of us that we could scarcely breathe. We
spent a horrible twenty-four hours there. There were men downstairs; women on the first floor. It was Saturday; it was as
though we had come to attend the service. Since no one could
go out, people were relieving themselves in a corner.

The following morning, we marched to the station, where a
convoy of cattle wagons was waiting. The Hungarian police
made us get in—eighty people in each car. We were left a few
loaves of bread and some buckets of water. The bars at the window were checked, to see that they were not loose. Then the
cars were sealed. In each car one person was placed in charge.
If anyone escaped, he would be shot.

Two Gestapo officers strolled about on the platform, smiling:
all things considered, everything had gone off very well.

A prolonged whistle split the air. The wheels began to grind.
We were on our way.

2

LYING down was out of the question, and we were only able to sit by deciding to take turns. There was very little air. The lucky ones who happened to be near a window could see the blossoming countryside roll by.

After two days of traveling, we began to be tortured by thirst. Then the heat became unbearable.

Free from all social constraint, young people gave way openly to instinct, taking advantage of the darkness to flirt in our midst, without caring about anyone else, as though they were alone in the world. The rest pretended not to notice anything.

We still had a few provisions left. But we never ate enough to satisfy our hunger. To save was our rule; to save up for tomorrow. Tomorrow might be worse.

The train stopped at Kaschau, a little town on the Czechoslovak frontier. We realized then that we were not going to stay in Hungary. Our eyes were opened, but too late.

The door of the car slid open. A German officer, accompanied by a Hungarian lieutenant-interpreter, came up and introduced himself.

"From this moment, you come under the authority of the German army. Those of you who still have gold, silver, or watches in your possession must give them up now. Anyone who is later found to have kept anything will be shot on the spot. Secondly, anyone who feels ill may go to the hospital car. That's all."

The Hungarian lieutenant went among us with a basket and collected the last possessions from those who no longer wished to taste the bitterness of terror.

"There are eighty of you in this wagon," added the German officer. "If anyone is missing, you'll all be shot, like dogs. . . ."

They disappeared. The doors were closed. We were caught in a trap, right up to our necks. The doors were nailed up; the way back was finally cut off. The world was a cattle wagon hermetically sealed.

We had a woman with us named Madame Schächter. She was about fifty; her ten-year-old son was with her, crouched in a corner. Her husband and two eldest sons had been deported with the first transport by mistake. The separation had completely broken her.

I knew her well. A quiet woman with tense, burning eyes, she had often been to our house. Her husband, who was a pious man, spent his days and nights in study, and it was she who worked to support the family.

Madame Schächter had gone out of her mind. On the first day of the journey she had already begun to moan and to keep asking why she had been separated from her family. As time went on, her cries grew hysterical.

On the third night, while we slept, some of us sitting one against the other and some standing, a piercing cry split the silence:

"Fire! I can see a fire! I can see a fire!"

There was a moment's panic. Who was it who had cried out? It was Madame Schächter. Standing in the middle of the wagon, in the pale light from the windows, she looked like a withered tree in a cornfield. She pointed her arm toward the window, screaming:

"Look! Look at it! Fire! A terrible fire! Mercy! *Oh, that fire!*"

Some of the men pressed up against the bars. There was nothing there; only the darkness.

The shock of this terrible awakening stayed with us for a long time. We still trembled from it. With every groan of the wheels on the rail, we felt that an abyss was about to open beneath our bodies. Powerless to still our own anguish, we tried to console ourselves:

"She's mad, poor soul. . . ."

Someone had put a damp cloth on her brow, to calm her, but still her screams went on:

"Fire! Fire!"

Her little boy was crying, hanging onto her skirt, trying to take hold of her hands. "It's all right, Mummy! There's nothing there. . . . Sit down. . . ." This shook me even more than his mother's screams had done.

Some women tried to calm her. "You'll find your husband and your sons again . . . in a few days. . . ."

She continued to scream, breathless, her voice broken by sobs. "Jews, listen to me! I can see a fire! There are huge flames! It is a furnace!"

It was as though she were possessed by an evil spirit which spoke from the depths of her being.

We tried to explain it away, more to calm ourselves and to recover our own breath than to comfort her. "She must be very thirsty, poor thing! That's why she keeps talking about a fire devouring her."

But it was in vain. Our terror was about to burst the sides of the train. Our nerves were at breaking point. Our flesh was creeping. It was as though madness were taking possession of us all. We could stand it no longer. Some of the young men forced her to sit down, tied her up, and put a gag in her mouth. Silence again. The little boy sat down by his mother, crying. I had begun to breathe normally again. We could hear the wheels churning out that monotonous rhythm of a train traveling through the night. We could begin to doze, to rest, to dream. . . .

An hour or two went by like this. Then another scream took our breath away. The woman had broken loose from her bonds and was crying out more loudly than ever:

"Look at the fire! Flames, flames everywhere. . . ."

Once more the young men tied her up and gagged her. They even struck her. People encouraged them:

"Make her be quiet! She's mad! Shut her up! She's not the only one. She can keep her mouth shut. . . ."

They struck her several times on the head—blows that might have killed her. Her little boy clung to her; he did not cry out; he did not say a word. He was not even weeping now.

An endless night. Toward dawn, Madame Schächter calmed down. Crouched in her corner, her bewildered gaze scouring the emptiness, she could no longer see us.

She stayed like that all through the day, dumb, absent, isolated among us. As soon as night fell, she began to scream: "There's a fire over there!" She would point at a spot in space, always the same one. They were tired of hitting her. The heat, the thirst, the pestilential stench, the suffocating lack of air—these were as nothing compared with these screams which tore us to shreds. A few days more and we should all have started to scream too.

But we had reached a station. Those who were next to the windows told us its name:

"Auschwitz."

No one had ever heard that name.

The train did not start up again. The afternoon passed slowly. Then the wagon doors slid open. Two men were allowed to get down to fetch water.

When they came back, they told us that, in exchange for a gold watch, they had discovered that this was the last stop. We would be getting out here. There was a labor camp. Conditions were good. Families would not be split up. Only the young people would go to work in the factories. The old men and invalids would be kept occupied in the fields.

The barometer of confidence soared. Here was a sudden release from the terrors of the previous nights. We gave thanks to God.

Madame Schächter stayed in her corner, wilted, dumb, indifferent to the general confidence. Her little boy stroked her hand.

As dusk fell, darkness gathered inside the wagon. We started to eat our last provisions. At ten in the evening, everyone was looking for a convenient position in which to sleep for a while, and soon we were all asleep. Suddenly:

"The fire! The furnace! Look, over there! . . ."

Waking with a start, we rushed to the window. Yet again we had believed her, even if only for a moment. But there was nothing outside save the darkness of night. With shame in our souls, we went back to our places, gnawed by fear, in spite of ourselves. As she continued to scream, they began to hit her again, and it was with the greatest difficulty that they silenced her.

The man in charge of our wagon called a German officer who was walking about on the platform, and asked him if Madame Schächter could be taken to the hospital car.

"You must be patient," the German replied. "She'll be taken there soon."

Toward eleven o'clock, the train began to move. We pressed against the windows. The convoy was moving slowly. A quarter of an hour later, it slowed down again. Through the windows we could see barbed wire; we realized that this must be the camp.

We had forgotten the existence of Madame Schächter. Suddenly, we heard terrible screams:

"Jews, look! Look through the window! Flames! Look!"

And as the train stopped, we saw this time that flames were gushing out of a tall chimney into the black sky.

Madame Schächter was silent herself. Once more she had become dumb, indifferent, absent, and had gone back to her corner.

We looked at the flames in the darkness. There was an abominable odor floating in the air. Suddenly, our doors opened. Some odd-looking characters, dressed in striped shirts and black trousers leapt into the wagon. They held electric torches and truncheons. They began to strike out to right and left, shouting:

"Everybody get out! Everyone out of the wagon! Quickly!"

We jumped out. I threw a last glance toward Madame Schächter. Her little boy was holding her hand.

In front of us flames. In the air that smell of burning flesh. It must have been about midnight. We had arrived—at Birkenau, reception center for Auschwitz.

3

THE cherished objects we had brought with us thus far were left behind in the train, and with them, at last, our illusions.

Every two yards or so an SS man held his tommy gun trained on us. Hand in hand we followed the crowd.

An SS noncommissioned officer came to meet us, a truncheon in his hand. He gave the order:

"Men to the left! Women to the right!"

Eight words spoken quietly, indifferently, without emotion. Eight short, simple words. Yet that was the moment when I parted from my mother. I had not had time to think, but already I felt the pressure of my father's hand: we were alone. For a part of a second I glimpsed my mother and my sisters moving away to the right. Tzipora held Mother's hand. I saw them disappear into the distance; my mother was stroking my sister's fair hair, as though to protect her, while I walked on with my father and the other men. And I did not know that in that place, at that moment, I was parting from my mother and Tzipora forever. I went on walking. My father held onto my hand.

Behind me, an old man fell to the ground. Near him was an SS man, putting his revolver back in its holster.

My hand shifted on my father's arm. I had one thought—not to lose him. Not to be left alone.

The SS officers gave the order:

"Form fives!"

Commotion. At all costs we must keep together.

"Here, kid, how old are you?"

It was one of the prisoners who asked me this. I could not see his face, but his voice was tense and weary.

"I'm not quite fifteen yet."

"No. Eighteen."

"But I'm not," I said. "Fifteen."

"Fool. Listen to what *I* say."

Then he questioned my father, who replied:

"Fifty."

The other grew more furious than ever.

"No, not fifty. Forty. Do you understand? Eighteen and forty."

He disappeared into the night shadows. A second man came up, spitting oaths at us.

"What have you come here for, you sons of bitches? What are you doing here, eh?"

Someone dared to answer him.

"What do you think? Do you suppose we've come here for our own pleasure? Do you think we asked to come?"

A little more, and the man would have killed him.

"You shut your trap, you filthy swine, or I'll squash you right now! You'd have done better to have hanged yourselves where you were than come here. Didn't you know what was in store for you at Auschwitz? Haven't you heard about it? In 1944?"

No, we had not heard. No one had told us. He could not believe his ears. His tone of voice became increasingly brutal.

"Do you see that chimney over there? See it? Do you see those flames? (Yes, we did see the flames.) Over there—that's where you're going to be taken. That's your grave, over there. Haven't you realized it yet? You dumb bastards, don't you understand anything? You're going to be burned. Frizzled away. Turned into ashes."

He was growing hysterical in his fury. We stayed motionless, petrified. Surely it was all a nightmare? An unimaginable nightmare?

I heard murmurs around me.

"We've got to do something. We can't let ourselves be killed. We can't go like beasts to the slaughter. We've got to revolt."

There were a few sturdy young fellows among us. They had knives on them, and they tried to incite the others to throw themselves on the armed guards.

One of the young men cried:

"Let the world learn of the existence of Auschwitz. Let everybody hear about it, while they can still escape. . . ."

But the older ones begged their children not to do anything foolish:

"You must never lose faith, even when the sword hangs over your head. That's the teaching of our sages. . . ."

The wind of revolt died down. We continued our march toward the square. In the middle stood the notorious Dr. Mengele (a typical SS officer: a cruel face, but not devoid of intelligence, and wearing a monocle); a conductor's baton in his hand, he was standing among the other officers. The baton moved unremittingly, sometimes to the right, sometimes to the left.

I was already in front of him:

"How old are you?" he asked, in an attempt at a paternal tone of voice.

"Eighteen." My voice was shaking.

"Are you in good health?"

"Yes."

"What's your occupation?"

Should I say that I was a student?

"Farmer," I heard myself say.

This conversation cannot have lasted more than a few seconds. It had seemed like an eternity to me.

The baton moved to the left. I took half a step forward. I wanted to see first where they were sending my father. If he went to the right, I would go after him.

The baton once again pointed to the left for him too. A weight was lifted from my heart.

We did not yet know which was the better side, right or left; which road led to prison and which to the crematory. But for the moment I was happy; I was near my father. Our procession continued to move slowly forward.

Another prisoner came up to us:

"Satisfied?"

"Yes," someone replied.

"Poor devils, you're going to the crematory."

He seemed to be telling the truth. Not far from us, flames were leaping up from a ditch, gigantic flames. They were burning something. A lorry drew up at the pit and delivered its load—little children. Babies! Yes, I saw it—saw it with my own eyes . . . those children in the flames. (Is it surprising that I could not sleep after that? Sleep had fled from my eyes.)

So this was where we were going. A little farther on was another and larger ditch for adults.

I pinched my face. Was I still alive? Was I awake? I could not believe it. How could it be possible for them to burn people, children, and for the world to keep silent? No, none of this could be true. It was a nightmare. . . . Soon I should wake with a start, my heart pounding, and find myself back in the bedroom of my childhood, among my books. . . .

My father's voice drew me from my thoughts:

"It's a shame . . . a shame that you couldn't have gone with your mother. . . . I saw several boys of your age going with their mothers. . . ."

His voice was terribly sad. I realized that he did not want to see what they were going to do to me. He did not want to see the burning of his only son.

My forehead was bathed in cold sweat. But I told him that I did not believe that they could burn people in our age, that humanity would never tolerate it. . . .

"Humanity? Humanity is not concerned with us. Today anything

is allowed. Anything is possible, even these crematories. . . ."
His voice was choking.

"Father," I said, "if that is so, I don't want to wait here. I'm
going to run to the electric wire. That would be better than slow
agony in the flames."

He did not answer. He was weeping. His body was shaken
convulsively. Around us, everyone was weeping. Someone began
to recite the Kaddish, the prayer for the dead. I do not know if it
has ever happened before, in the long history of the Jews, that
people have ever recited the prayer for the dead for themselves.

"*Yitgadal veyitkadach shmé raba.* . . . May His Name be
blessed and magnified. . . ." whispered my father.

For the first time, I felt revolt rise up in me. Why should I
bless His name? The Eternal, Lord of the Universe, the All-
Powerful and Terrible, was silent. What had I to thank Him for?

We continued our march. We were gradually drawing closer to
the ditch, from which an infernal heat was rising. Still twenty
steps to go. If I wanted to bring about my own death, this was the
moment. Our line had now only fifteen paces to cover. I bit my lips
so that my father would not hear my teeth chattering. Ten steps
still. Eight. Seven. We marched slowly on, as though following a
hearse at our own funeral. Four steps more. Three steps. There it
was now, right in front of us, the pit and its flames. I gathered all
that was left of my strength, so that I could break from the ranks
and throw myself upon the barbed wire. In the depths of my heart,
I bade farewell to my father, to the whole universe; and, in spite of
myself, the words formed themselves and issued in a whisper from
my lips: *Yitgadal veyitkadach shmé raba.* . . . May His name be
blessed and magnified. . . . My heart was bursting. The moment
had come. I was face to face with the Angel of Death. . . .

No. Two steps from the pit we were ordered to turn to the left
and made to go into a barracks.

I pressed my father's hand. He said:

"Do you remember Madame Schächter, in the train?"

Never shall I forget that night, the first night in camp, which
has turned my life into one long night, seven times cursed and
seven times sealed. Never shall I forget that smoke. Never shall I
forget the little faces of the children, whose bodies I saw turned
into wreaths of smoke beneath a silent blue sky.

Never shall I forget those flames which consumed my faith
forever.

Never shall I forget that nocturnal silence which deprived me,
for all eternity, of the desire to live. Never shall I forget those

moments which murdered my God and my soul and turned my dreams to dust. Never shall I forget these things, even if I am condemned to live as long as God Himself. Never.

The barracks we had been made to go into was very long. In the roof were some blue-tinged skylights. The antechamber of Hell must look like this. So many crazed men, so many cries, so much bestial brutality!

There were dozens of prisoners to receive us, truncheons in their hands, striking out anywhere, at anyone, without reason. Orders:

"Strip! Fast! *Los!* Keep only your belts and shoes in your hands. . . ."

We had to throw our clothes at one end of the barracks. There was already a great heap there. New suits and old, torn coats, rags. For us, this was the true equality: nakedness. Shivering with the cold.

Some SS officers moved about in the room, looking for strong men. If they were so keen on strength, perhaps one should try and pass oneself off as sturdy? My father thought the reverse. It was better not to draw attention to oneself. Our fate would then be the same as the others. (Later, we were to learn that he was right. Those who were selected that day were enlisted in the *Sonder-Kommando,* the unit which worked in the crematories. Bela Katz—son of a big tradesman from our town—had arrived at Birkenau with the first transport, a week before us. When he heard of our arrival, he managed to get word to us that, having been chosen for his strength, he had himself put his father's body into the crematory oven.)

Blows continued to rain down.

"To the barber!"

Belt and shoes in hand, I let myself be dragged off to the barbers. They took our hair off with clippers, and shaved off all the hair on our bodies. The same thought buzzed all the time in my head—not to be separated from my father.

Freed from the hands of the barbers, we began to wander in the crowd, meeting friends and acquaintances. These meetings filled us with joy—yes, joy—"Thank God! You're still alive!"

But others were crying. They used all their remaining strength in weeping. Why had they let themselves be brought here? Why couldn't they have died in their beds? Sobs choked their voices.

Suddenly, someone threw his arms round my neck in an embrace: Yechiel, brother of the rabbi of Sighet. He was sobbing bitterly. I thought he was weeping with joy at still being alive.

"Don't cry, Yechiel," I said. "Don't waste your tears. . . ."

"Not cry? We're on the threshold of death. . . . Soon we shall have crossed over. . . . Don't you understand? How could I not cry?"

Through the blue-tinged skylights I could see the darkness gradually fading. I had ceased to feel fear. And then I was overcome by an inhuman weariness.

Those absent no longer touched even the surface of our memories. We still spoke of them—"Who knows what may have become of them?"—but we had little concern for their fate. We were incapable of thinking of anything at all. Our senses were blunted; everything was blurred as in a fog. It was no longer possible to grasp anything. The instincts of self-preservation, of self-defense, of pride, had all deserted us. In one ultimate moment of lucidity it seemed to me that we were damned souls wandering in the half-world, souls condemned to wander through space till the generations of man came to an end, seeking their redemption, seeking oblivion—without hope of finding it.

Toward five o'clock in the morning, we were driven out of the barracks. The Kapos beat us once more, but I had ceased to feel any pain from their blows. An icy wind enveloped us. We were naked, our shoes and belts in our hands. The command: "Run!" And we ran. After a few minutes of racing, a new barracks.

A barrel of petrol at the entrance. Disinfection. Everyone was soaked in it. Then a hot shower. At high speed. As we came out from the water, we were driven outside. More running. Another barracks, the store. Very long tables. Mountains of prison clothes. On we ran. As we passed, trousers, tunic, shirt, and socks were thrown to us.

Within a few seconds, we had ceased to be men. If the situation had not been tragic, we should have roared with laughter. Such outfits! Meir Katz, a giant, had a child's trousers, and Stern, a thin little chap, a tunic which completely swamped him. We immediately began the necessary exchanges.

I glanced at my father. How he had changed! His eyes had grown dim. I would have liked to speak to him, but I did not know what to say.

The night was gone. The morning star was shining in the sky. I too had become a completely different person. The student of the Talmud, the child that I was, had been consumed in the flames. There remained only a shape that looked like me. A dark flame had entered into my soul and devoured it.

So much had happened within such a few hours that I had lost all sense of time. When had we left our houses? And the ghetto? And the train? Was it only a week? One night—*one single night?*

How long had we been standing like this in the icy wind? An hour? Simply an hour? Sixty minutes?

Surely it was a dream.

Not far from us there were some prisoners at work. Some were digging holes, others carrying sand. None of them so much as glanced at us. We were so many dried-up trees in the heart of a desert. Behind me, some people were talking. I had not the slightest desire to listen to what they were saying, to know who was talking or what they were talking about. No one dared to raise his voice, though there was no supervisor near us. People whispered. Perhaps it was because of the thick smoke which poisoned the air and took one by the throat. . . .

We were made to go into a new barracks, in the "gypsies' camp." In ranks of five.

"And now stay where you are!"

There was no floor. A roof and four walls. Our feet sank into the mud.

Another spell of waiting began. I went to sleep standing up. I dreamed of a bed, of my mother's caress. And I woke up: I was standing, my feet in the mud. Some people collapsed and lay where they were. Others cried:

"Are you mad? We've been told to stay standing. Do you want to bring trouble on us all?"

As if all the trouble in the world had not descended already upon our heads! Gradually, we all sat down in the mud. But we had to jump up constantly, every time a Kapo came in to see if anybody had a pair of new shoes. If so, they had to be given up to him. It was no use opposing this: blows rained down and in the final reckoning you had lost your shoes anyway.

I had new shoes myself. But as they were coated with a thick layer of mud, no one had noticed them. I thanked God, in an improvised prayer, for having created mud in His infinite and wonderful universe.

Suddenly the silence grew oppressive. An SS officer had come in and, with him, the odor of the Angel of Death. We stared fixedly at his fleshy lips. From the middle of the barracks, he harangued us:

"You're in a concentration camp. At Auschwitz. . . ."

A pause. He observed the effect his words had produced. His face has stayed in my memory to this day. A tall man, about thirty, with crime inscribed upon his brow and in the pupils of his eyes. He looked us over as if we were a pack of leprous dogs hanging onto our lives.

"Remember this," he went on. "Remember it forever. Engrave it into your minds. You are at Auschwitz. And Auschwitz is not a convalescent home. It's a concentration camp. Here, you have got to work. If not, you will go straight to the furnace. To the crematory. Work or the crematory—the choice is in your hands."

We had already lived through so much that night, we thought nothing could frighten us any more. But his clipped words made us tremble. Here the word "furnace" was not a word empty of meaning: it floated on the air, mingling with the smoke. It was perhaps the only word which did have any real meaning here. He left the barracks. Kapos appeared, crying:

"All skilled workers—locksmiths, electricians, watchmakers— one step forward!"

The rest of us were made to go to another barracks, a stone one this time. With permission to sit down. A gypsy deportee was in charge of us.

My father was suddenly seized with colic. He got up and went toward the gypsy, asking politely, in German:

"Excuse me, can you tell me where the lavatories are?"

The gypsy looked him up and down slowly, from head to foot. As if he wanted to convince himself that this man addressing him was really a creature of flesh and bone, a living being with a body and a belly. Then, as if he had suddenly woken up from a heavy doze, he dealt my father such a clout that he fell to the ground, crawling back to his place on all fours.

I did not move. What had happened to me? My father had just been struck, before my very eyes, and I had not flickered an eyelid. I had looked on and said nothing. Yesterday, I should have sunk my nails into the criminal's flesh. Had I changed so much, then? So quickly? Now remorse began to gnaw at me. I thought only: I shall never forgive them for that. My father must have guessed my feelings. He whispered in my ear, "It doesn't hurt." His cheek still bore the red mark of the man's hand.

"Everyone outside!"

Ten gypsies had come and joined our supervisor. Whips and truncheons cracked round me. My feet were running without my being aware of it. I tried to hide from the blows behind the others. The spring sunshine.

"Form fives!"

The prisoners whom I had noticed in the morning were working at the side. There was no guard near them, only the shadow of the chimney. . . . Dazed by the sunshine and by my reverie, I felt someone tugging at my sleeve. It was my father. "Come on, my boy."

We marched on. Doors opened and closed again. On we went between the electric wires. At each step, a white placard with a death's head on it stared us in the face. A caption: "Warning. Danger of death." Mockery: was there a single place here where you were not in danger of death?

The gypsies stopped near another barracks. They were replaced by SS, who surrounded us. Revolvers, machine guns, police dogs.

The march had lasted half an hour. Looking around me, I noticed that the barbed wires were behind us. We had left the camp.

It was a beautiful April day. The fragrance of spring was in the air. The sun was setting in the west.

But we had been marching for only a few moments when we saw the barbed wire of another camp. An iron door with this inscription over it:

"Work is liberty!"

Auschwitz.

First impression: this was better than Birkenau. There were two-storied buildings of concrete instead of wooden barracks. There were little gardens here and there. We were led to one of these prison blocks. Seated on the ground by the entrance, we began another session of waiting. Every now and then, someone was made to go in. These were the showers, a compulsory formality at the entrance to all these camps. Even if you were simply passing from one to the other several times a day, you still had to go through the baths every time.

After coming out from the hot water, we stayed shivering in the night air. Our clothes had been left behind in the other block, and we had been promised other outfits.

Toward midnight, we were told to run.

"Faster," shouted our guards. "The faster you run, the sooner you can go to bed."

After a few minutes of this mad race we arrived in front of another block. The prisoner in charge was waiting for us. He was a young Pole, who smiled at us. He began to talk to us, and, despite our weariness, we listened patiently.

"Comrades, you're in the concentration camp of Auschwitz. There's a long road of suffering ahead of you. But don't lose courage. You've already escaped the gravest danger: selection. So now, muster your strength, and don't lose heart. We shall all see the day of liberation. Have faith in life. Above all else, have faith. Drive out despair, and you will keep death away from yourselves. Hell is not for eternity. And now, a prayer—or rather, a piece of advice: let there be comradeship among you. We are all brothers, and we are all suffering the same fate. The same smoke floats over all our heads. Help one another. It is the only way to survive. Enough said. You're tired. Listen. You're in Block 17. I am responsible for keeping order here. Anyone with a complaint against anyone else can come and see me. That's all. You can go to bed. Two people to a bunk. Good night." The first human words.

No sooner had we climbed into the bunks than we fell into a deep sleep.

The next morning, the "veteran" prisoners treated us without brutality. We went to the wash place. We were given new clothes. We were brought black coffee.

We left the block at about ten o'clock, so that it could be cleaned. Outside the sunshine warmed us. Our morale was much improved. We were feeling the benefit of a night's sleep. Friends met each other, exchanged a few sentences. We talked of everything, except those who had disappeared. The general opinion was that the war was about to end.

At about noon they brought us soup: a plate of thick soup for each person. Tormented though I was by hunger, I refused to touch it. I was still the spoiled child I had always been. My father swallowed my ration.

In the shade of the block, we then had a little siesta. He must have been lying, that SS officer in the muddy barracks. Auschwitz was in fact a rest home. . . .

In the afternoon we were made to line up. Three prisoners brought a table and some medical instruments. With the left sleeve rolled up, each person passed in front of the table. The three "veterans," with needles in their hands, engraved a number on our left arms. I became A-7713. After that I had no other name.

At dusk, roll call. The working units came back. Near the door, the band was playing military marches. Tens of thousands of prisoners stood in rows while the SS checked their numbers.

After roll call, the prisoners from all the blocks scattered to look for friends, relatives, and neighbors who had arrived in the last convoy.

Days passed. In the morning, black coffee. At noon, soup. (By the third day I was eating any kind of soup hungrily.) At six p.m., roll call. Then bread and something. At nine o'clock, bed.

We had already been eight days at Auschwitz. It was during roll call. We were not expecting anything except the sound of the bell which would announce the end of roll call. I suddenly heard someone passing between the rows asking, "Which of you is Wiesel of Sighet?"

The man looking for us was a bespectacled little fellow with a wrinkled, wizened face. My father answered him.

"I'm Wiesel of Sighet."

The little man looked at him for a long while, with his eyes narrowed.

"You don't recognize me—you don't recognize me. I'm a relative of yours. Stein. Have you forgotten me already? Stein! Stein of Antwerp. Reizel's husband. Your wife was Reizel's aunt. She often used to write to us . . . and such letters!"

My father had not recognized him. He must scarcely have known him, since my father was always up to his neck in the affairs of the Jewish community, and much less well versed in family matters. He was always elsewhere, lost in his thoughts. (Once a cousin came to see us at Sighet. She had been staying with us and eating at our table for over a fortnight before my father noticed her presence for the first time.) No, he could not have remembered Stein. As for me, I recognized him at once. I had known his wife Reizel before she left for Belgium.

He said, "I was deported in 1942. I heard that a transport had come in from your region, and I came to find you. I thought perhaps you might have news of Reizel and my little boys. They stayed behind in Antwerp. . . ."

I knew nothing about them. Since 1940, my mother had not had a single letter from them. But I lied.

"Yes, my mother's had news from your family. Reizel is very well. The children too. . . ."

He wept with joy. He would have liked to stay longer, to learn more details, to drink in the good news, but an SS came up, and he had to go, calling to us that he would be back the next day.

The bell gave us the signal to disperse. We went to get our

evening meal of bread and margarine. I was dreadfully hungry and swallowed my ration on the spot.

My father said, "You don't want to eat it all at once. Tomorrow's another day. . . ."

And seeing that his advice had come too late and that there was nothing left of my ration, he did not even begin his own.

"Personally, I'm not hungry," he said.

We stayed at Auschwitz for three weeks. We had nothing to do. We slept a great deal in the afternoon and at night.

The only worry was to avoid moves, to stay here as long as possible. It was not difficult; it was simply a matter of never putting oneself down as a skilled worker. Laborers were being kept till the end.

At the beginning of the third week, the prisoner in charge of our block was deprived of his office, being considered too humane. Our new head was savage, and his assistants were real monsters. The good days were over. We began to wonder if it would not be better to let oneself be chosen for the next move.

Stein, our relation from Antwerp, continued to visit us, and from time to time he would bring a half ration of bread.

"Here, this is for you, Eliezer."

Every time he came, there would be tears running down his face, congealing there, freezing. He would often say to my father:

"Take care of your son. He's very weak and dried up. Look after him well, to avoid the selection. Eat! It doesn't matter what or when. Eat everything you can. The weak don't hang about for long here. . . ."

And he was so thin himself, so dried up, so weak. . . .

"The only thing that keeps me alive," he used to say, "is that Reizel and the children are still alive. If it wasn't for them, I couldn't keep going."

He came toward us one evening, his face radiant.

"A transport's just come in from Antwerp. I'm going to see them tomorrow. They'll be sure to have news."

He went off.

We were not to see him again. He had had news. Real news.

In the evening, lying on our beds, we would try to sing some of the Hasidic melodies, and Akiba Drumer would break our hearts with his deep, solemn voice.

Some talked of God, of his mysterious ways, of the sins of the Jewish people, and of their future deliverance. But I had ceased to pray. How I sympathized with Job! I did not deny God's existence, but I doubted His absolute justice.

Akiba Drumer said: "God is testing us. He wants to find out whether we can dominate our base instincts and kill the Satan within us. We have no right to despair. And if he punishes us relentlessly, it's a sign that He loves us all the more."

Hersch Genud, well versed in the cabbala, spoke of the end of the world and the coming of Messiah.

Only occasionally during these conversations did the thought occur to me: "Where is my mother at this moment? And Tzipora . . . ?"

"Your mother is still a young woman," said my father on one occasion. "She must be in a labor camp. And Tzipora's a big girl now, isn't she? She must be in a camp, too."

How we should have liked to believe it. We pretended, for what if the other one should still be believing it?

All the skilled workers had already been sent to other camps. There were only about a hundred of us ordinary laborers left.

"It's your turn today," said the secretary of the block. "You're going with the next transport."

At ten o'clock we were given our daily ration of bread. We were surrounded by about ten SS. On the door the plaque: *"Work is liberty."* We were counted. And then, there we were, right out in the country on the sunny road. In the sky a few little white clouds.

We walked slowly. The guards were in no hurry. We were glad of this. As we went through the villages, many of the Germans stared at us without surprise. They had probably already seen quite a few of these processions.

On the way, we met some young German girls. The guards began to tease them. The girls giggled, pleased. They let themselves be kissed and tickled, exploding with laughter. They were all laughing and joking and shouting blandishments at one another for a good part of the way. During this time, at least we did not have to endure either shouts or blows from the rifle butt.

At the end of four hours, we reached our new camp: Buna. The iron gate closed behind us.

4

THE camp looked as though it had suffered an epidemic: empty and dead. There were just a few well-clad prisoners walking about between the blocks.

Of course, we had to go through the showers first. The head of our camp joined us there. He was a strong, well-built, broad-shouldered man: bull neck, thick lips, frizzled hair. He looked kind. A smile shone from time to time in his gray-blue eyes. Our convoy included a few children ten and twelve years old. The officer took an interest in them and gave orders for them to be brought food.

After we had been given new clothes, we were installed in two tents. We had to wait to be enlisted in the labor units, then we could pass into the block.

That evening, the labor units came back from the work yards. Roll call. We began to look for familiar faces, to seek information, to question the veteran prisoners about which labor unit was the best, which block one should try to get into. The prisoners all agreed, saying, "Buna's a very good camp. You can stand it. The important thing is not to get transferred to the building unit. . . ."

As if the choice were in our own hands.

The head of our tent was a German. An assassin's face, fleshy lips, hands like a wolf's paws. He was so fat he could hardly move. Like the leader of the camp, he loved children. As soon as we arrived, he had brought them bread, soup, and margarine. (Actually, this was not disinterested affection: there was a considerable traffic in children among homosexuals here, I learned later.)

The head told us: "You're staying here three days in quarantine. Then you're going to work. Tomorrow, medical inspection."

One of his assistants—a hard-faced boy, with hooligan's eyes—came up to me:

"Do you want to get into a good unit?"

"I certainly do. But on one condition: I want to stay with my father."

"All right," he said. "I can arrange that. For a small consideration: your shoes. I'll give you some others."

I refused to give him my shoes. They were all I had left.

"I'll give you an extra ration of bread and margarine."

He was very keen on my shoes; but I did not give them up to him. (Later on they were taken from me just the same. But in exchange for nothing this time.)

Medical examination in the open air in the early hours of the morning, before three doctors seated on a bench.

The first barely examined me at all. He was content merely to ask:

"Are you in good health?"

Who would have dared say anything to the contrary?

The dentist, on the other hand, seemed most conscientious: he would order us to open our mouths wide. Actually he was not looking for decayed teeth, but gold ones. Anyone who had gold in his mouth had his number added to a list. I myself had a gold crown.

The first three days passed by rapidly. On the fourth day, at dawn, when we were standing in front of the tent, the Kapos appeared. Then each began to choose the men who suited him:

"You . . . you . . . you and you. . . ." They pointed a finger, as though choosing cattle or merchandise.

We followed our Kapo, a young man. He made us stop at the entrance to the first block, near the door of the camp. This was the orchestra block. "Go in," he ordered. We were surprised. What had we to do with music?

The band played a military march, always the same one. Dozens of units left for the workyards, in step. The Kapos beat time: "Left, right, left, right."

Some SS officers, pen and paper in hand, counted the men as they went out. The band went on playing the same march until the last unit had gone by. Then the conductor's baton was still. The band stopped dead, and the Kapos yelled:

"Form fives!"

We left the camp without music, but in step: we still had the sound of the march in our ears.

"Left, right! Left, right!"

We started talking to the musicians next to us.

We drew up in ranks of five, with the musicians. They were nearly all Jews: Juliek, a bespectacled Pole with a cynical smile on his pale face; Louis, a distinguished violinist who came from Holland—he complained that they would not let him play Beethoven: Jews were not allowed to play German music; Hans, a lively young Berliner. The foreman was a Pole, Franek, a former student from Warsaw.

Juliek explained to me: "We work in a warehouse for electrical equipment, not far from here. The work isn't in the least difficult or dangerous. But Idek, the Kapo, has bouts of madness now and then, when it's best to keep out of his way."

"You're lucky, son," smiled Hans. "You've landed in a good unit. . . ."

Ten minutes later, we were in front of the warehouse. A German employee, a civilian, the *meister*, came to meet us. He paid us about as much attention as a dealer might who was just receiving a delivery of old rags.

Our comrades had been right; the work was not difficult. Sitting on the ground, we had to count bolts, bulbs, and small electrical fittings. The Kapo explained to us at great length the vast importance of our work, warning us that anyone found slacking would have him to reckon with. My new comrades reassured me.

"There's nothing to be scared of. He has to say that because of the *meister*."

There were a number of Polish civilians there, and a few French women, who were casting friendly glances at the musicians.

Franek, the foreman, put me in a corner. "Don't kill yourself; there's no hurry. But mind an SS man doesn't catch you unawares."

"Please . . . I would have liked to be by my father."

"All right. Your father'll be working here by your side."

We were lucky.

There were two boys attached to our group: Yossi and Tibi, two brothers. They were Czechs whose parents had been exterminated at Birkenau. They lived, body and soul, for each other.

They and I very soon became friends. Having once belonged to a Zionist youth organization, they knew innumerable Hebrew chants. Thus we would often hum tunes evoking the calm waters of Jordan and the majestic sanctity of Jerusalem. And we would often talk of Palestine. Their parents, like mine, had lacked the courage to wind up their affairs and emigrate while there was still time. We decided that, if we were granted our lives until the liberation, we would not stay in Europe a day longer. We would take the first boat for Haifa.

Still lost in his cabbalistic dreams, Akiba Drumer had discovered a verse in the Bible which, interpreted in terms of numerology, enabled him to predict that the deliverance was due within the coming weeks.

We had left the tents for the musicians' block. We were entitled to a blanket, a wash bowl, and a bar of soap. The head of the block was a German Jew.

It was good to be under a Jew. He was called Alphonse. A young man with an extraordinarily aged face, he was entirely devoted to the cause of "his" block. Whenever he could, he would organize a cauldron of soup for the young ones, the weak, all those who were dreaming more about an extra plateful than of liberty.

One day when we had just come back from the warehouse, I was sent for by the secretary of the block.

"A-7713?"

"That's me."

"After eating, you're to go to the dentist."

"But I haven't got toothache."

"After eating. Without fail."

I went to the hospital block. There were about twenty prisoners waiting in a queue in front of the door. It did not take long to discover why we had been summoned: it was for the extraction of our gold teeth.

The dentist, a Jew from Czechoslovakia, had a face like a death mask. When he opened his mouth, there was a horrible sight of yellow, decaying teeth. I sat in the chair and asked him humbly: "Please, what are you going to do?"

"Simply take out your gold crown," he replied, indifferently.

I had the idea of pretending to be ill.

"You couldn't wait a few days, Doctor? I don't feel very well. I've got a temperature. . . ."

He wrinkled his brow, thought for a moment, and took my pulse.

"All right, son. When you feel better, come back and see me. But don't wait till I send for you!"

I went to see him a week later. With the same excuse: I still did not feel any better. He did not seem to show any surprise, and I do not know if he believed me. He was probably glad to see that I had come back of my own accord, as I had promised. He gave me another reprieve.

A few days after this visit of mine, they closed the dentist's surgery, and he was thrown into prison. He was going to be hanged. It was alleged that he had been running a private traffic of his own in the prisoners' gold teeth. I did not feel any pity for him. I was even pleased about what had happened. I had saved my gold crown. It might be useful to me one day to buy something—bread or life. I now took little interest in anything except my daily plate of soup and my crust of stale bread. Bread, soup—these were my whole life. I was a body. Perhaps less than that even: a starved stomach. The stomach alone was aware of the passage of time.

At the warehouse I often worked next to a young French girl. We did not speak to one another, since she knew no German and I did not understand French.

She seemed to me to be a Jewess, though here she passed as Aryan. She was a forced labor deportee.

One day when Idek was seized with one of his fits of frenzy, I got in his way. He leapt on me, like a wild animal, hitting me in the chest, on the head, throwing me down and pulling me up again, his blows growing more and more violent, until I was covered with blood. As I was biting my lips to stop myself from screaming with pain, he must have taken my silence for defiance, for he went on hitting me even harder.

Suddenly he calmed down. As if nothing had happened, he sent me back to work. It was as though we had been taking part together in some game where we each had our role to play.

I dragged myself to my corner. I ached all over. I felt a cool hand wiping my blood-stained forehead. It was the French girl. She gave me her mournful smile and slipped a bit of bread into my hand. She looked into my eyes. I felt that she wanted to say something but was choked by fear. For a long moment she stayed like that, then her face cleared and she said to me in almost perfect German:

"Bite your lip, little brother. . . . Don't cry. Keep your anger and hatred for another day, for later on. The day will come, but not now. . . . Wait. Grit your teeth and wait. . . ."

Many years later, in Paris, I was reading my paper in the Metro. Facing me was a very beautiful woman with black hair and dreamy eyes. I had seen those eyes before somewhere. It was she.

"You don't recognize me?"

"I don't know you."

"In 1944 you were in Germany, at Buna, weren't you?"

"Yes. . . ."

"You used to work in the electrical warehouse. . . ."

"Yes," she said, somewhat disturbed. And then, after a moment's silence: "Wait a minute . . . I do remember. . . ."

"Idek, the Kapo . . . the little Jewish boy . . . your kind words. . . ."

We left the Metro together to sit down on the terrace of a café. We spent the whole evening reminiscing.

Before I parted from her, I asked her: "May I ask you a question?"

"I know what it will be—go on."

"What?"

"Am I Jewish . . . ? Yes, I am Jewish. From a religious family.

During the occupation I obtained forged papers and passed myself off as an Aryan. That's how I was enlisted in the forced labor groups, and when I was deported to Germany, I escaped the concentration camp. At the warehouse, no one knew I could speak German. That would have aroused suspicions. Saying those few words to you was risky: but I knew you wouldn't give me away. . . ."

Another time we had to load Diesel engines onto trains supervised by German soldiers. Idek's nerves were on edge. He was restraining himself with great difficulty. Suddenly, his frenzy broke out. The victim was my father.

"You lazy old devil!" Idek began to yell. "Do you call that work?"

And he began to beat him with an iron bar. At first my father crouched under the blows, then he broke in two, like a dry tree struck by lightning, and collapsed.

I had watched the whole scene without moving. I kept quiet. In fact I was thinking of how to get farther away so that I would not be hit myself. What is more, any anger I felt at that moment was directed, not against the Kapo, but against my father. I was angry with him, for not knowing how to avoid Idek's outbreak. That is what concentration camp life had made of me.

Franek, the foreman, one day noticed the gold-crowned tooth in my mouth.

"Give me your crown, kid."

I told him it was impossible, that I could not eat without it.

"What do they give you to eat, anyway?"

I found another answer; the crown had been put down on a list after the medical inspection. This could bring trouble on us both.

"If you don't give me your crown, you'll pay for it even more."

This sympathetic, intelligent youth was suddenly no longer the same person. His eyes gleamed with desire. I told him I had to ask my father's advice.

"Ask your father, kid. But I want an answer by tomorrow."

When I spoke to my father about it, he turned pale, was silent a long while, and then said:

"No, son, you mustn't do it."

"He'll take it out on us!"

"He won't dare."

But alas, Franek knew where to touch me; he knew my weak point. My father had never done military service, and he never succeeded in marching in step. Here, every time we moved from one place to another in a body, we marched in strict rhythm. This was Franek's chance to torment my father and to thrash him savagely every day. Left, right: punch! Left, right: clout!

I decided to give my father lessons myself, to teach him to change step, and to keep to the rhythm. We began to do exercises in front of our block. I would give the commands: "Left, right!" and my father would practice. Some of the prisoners began to laugh at us.

"Look at this little officer teaching the old chap to march. . . . Hey, general, how many rations of bread does the old boy give you for this?"

But my father's progress was still inadequate, and blows continued to rain down on him.

"So you still can't march in step, you lazy old devil?"

These scenes were repeated for two weeks. We could not stand any more. We had to give in. When the day came, Franek burst into wild laughter.

"I knew it, I knew quite well I would win. Better late than never. And because you've made me wait, that's going to cost you a ration of bread. A ration of bread for one of my pals, a famous dentist from Warsaw, so that he can take your crown out."

"What? *My* ration of bread so that you can have *my* crown?"

Franek grinned.

"What would you like then? Shall I break your teeth with my fist?"

That same evening, in the lavatory, the dentist from Warsaw pulled out my crowned tooth, with the aid of a rusty spoon.

Franek grew kinder. Occasionally, he even gave me extra soup. But that did not last long. A fortnight later, all the Poles were transferred to another camp. I had lost my crown for nothing.

A few days before the Poles left, I had a new experience.

It was a Sunday morning. Our unit did not need to go to work that day. But all the same Idek would not hear of our staying in the camp. We had to go to the warehouse. This sudden enthusiasm for work left us stunned.

At the warehouse, Idek handed us over to Franek, saying, "Do what you like. But do something. If not, you'll hear from me. . . ."

And he disappeared.

We did not know what to do. Tired of squatting down, we each in turn went for a walk through the warehouse, looking for a bit of bread some civilian might have left behind.

When I came to the back of the building, I heard a noise coming from a little room next door. I went up and saw Idek with a young Polish girl, half-naked, on a mattress. Then I understood why Idek had refused to let us stay in the camp. Moving a hundred prisoners so that he could lie with a girl! It struck me as so funny that I burst out laughing.

Idek leapt up, turned around, and saw me, while the girl tried to cover up her breasts. I wanted to run away, but my legs were glued to the ground. Idek seized me by the throat.

Speaking in a low voice, he said, "You wait and see, kid. . . . You'll soon find out what leaving your work's going to cost you. . . . You're going to pay for this pretty soon. . . . And now, go back to your place."

Half an hour before work usually ended, the Kapo collected together the whole unit. Roll call. Nobody knew what had happened. Roll call at this time of day? Here? But I knew. The Kapo gave a short speech.

"An ordinary prisoner has no right to meddle in other people's affairs. One of you does not seem to have understood this. I'm obliged, therefore, to make it very clear to him once and for all."

I felt the sweat run down my back.

"A-7713!"

I came forward.

"A box!" he ordered.

They brought him a box.

"Lie down on it! On your stomach!"

I obeyed.

Then I was aware of nothing but the strokes of the whip.

"One . . . two . . . ," he counted.

He took his time between each stroke. Only the first ones really hurt me. I could hear him counting:

"Ten . . . eleven . . ."

His voice was calm and reached me as through a thick wall.

"Twenty-three . . ."

Two more, I thought, half conscious. The Kapo waited.

"Twenty-four . . . twenty-five!"

It was over. But I did not realize it, for I had fainted. I felt myself come round as a bucket of cold water was thrown over me. I was still lying on the box. I could just vaguely make out the wet ground surrounding me. Then I heard someone cry out. It must have been the Kapo. I began to distinguish the words he was shouting.

"Get up!"

I probably made some movement to raise myself, because I felt myself falling back onto the box. How I longed to get up!

"Get up!" he yelled more loudly.

If only I could have answered him, at least; if only I could have told him that I could not move! But I could not manage to open my lips.

At Idek's command, two prisoners lifted me up and led me in front of him.

"Look me in the eye!"

I looked at him without seeing him. I was thinking of my father. He must have suffered more than I did.

"Listen to me, you bastard!" said Idek, coldly. "That's for your curiosity. You'll get five times more if you dare tell anyone what you saw! Understand?"

I nodded my head, once, ten times. I nodded ceaselessly, as if my head had decided to say yes without ever stopping.

One Sunday, when half of us—including my father—were at work, the rest—including myself—were in the block, taking advantage of the chance to stay in bed late in the morning.

At about ten o'clock, the air-raid sirens began to wail. An alert. The leaders of the block ran to assemble us inside, while the SS took refuge in the shelters. As it was relatively easy to escape during a warning—the guards left their lookout posts and the electric current was cut off in the barbed-wire fences—the SS had orders to kill anyone found outside the blocks.

Within a few minutes, the camp looked like an abandoned ship. Not a living soul on the paths. Near the kitchen, two cauldrons of steaming hot soup had been left, half full. Two cauldrons of soup, right in the middle of the path, with no one guarding them! A feast for kings, abandoned, supreme temptation! Hundreds of eyes looked at them, sparkling with desire. Two lambs, with a hundred wolves lying in wait for them. Two lambs without a shepherd—a gift. But who would dare?

Terror was stronger than hunger. Suddenly, we saw the door of Block 37 open imperceptibly. A man appeared, crawling like a worm in the direction of the cauldrons.

Hundreds of eyes followed his movements. Hundreds of men crawled with him, scraping their knees with his on the gravel. Every heart trembled, but with envy above all. This man had dared.

He reached the first cauldron. Hearts raced: he had succeeded. Jealousy consumed us, burned us up like straw. We never thought for a moment of admiring him. Poor hero, committing suicide for a ration of soup! In our thoughts we were murdering him.

Stretched out by the cauldron, he was now trying to raise himself up to the edge. Either from weakness or fear he stayed there, trying, no doubt, to muster up the last of his strength. At last he succeeded in hoisting himself onto the edge of the pot. For a moment, he seemed to be looking at himself, seeking his ghostlike reflection in the soup. Then, for no apparent reason, he let out a terrible cry, a rattle such as I had never heard before, and, his mouth open, thrust his head toward the still steaming liquid. We jumped at the explosion. Falling back onto the ground, his face stained with soup, the man writhed for a few seconds at the foot of the cauldron, then he moved no more.

Then we began to hear the airplanes. Almost at once, the barracks began to shake.

"They're bombing Buna!" someone shouted.

I thought of my father. But I was glad all the same. To see the whole works go up in fire—what revenge! We had heard so much talk about the defeats of German troops on various fronts, but we did not know how much to believe. This, today, was real!

We were not afraid. And yet, if a bomb had fallen on the blocks, it alone would have claimed hundreds of victims on the spot. But we were no longer afraid of death; at any rate, not of that death. Every bomb that exploded filled us with joy and gave us new confidence in life.

The raid lasted over an hour. If it could only have lasted ten times ten hours! . . . Then silence fell once more. The last sound of an American plane was lost on the wind, and we found ourselves back again in the cemetery. A great trail of black smoke was rising up on the horizon. The sirens began to wail once more. It was the end of the alert.

Everyone came out of the blocks. We filled our lungs with the fire- and smoke-laden air, and our eyes shone with hope. A bomb had fallen in the middle of the camp, near the assembly point, but it had not gone off. We had to take it outside the camp.

The head of the camp, accompanied by his assistant and the chief Kapo, made a tour of inspection along the paths. The raid had left traces of terror on his face.

Right in the middle of the camp lay the body of the man with the soup-stained face, the only victim. The cauldrons were taken back into the kitchen.

The SS had gone back to their lookout posts, behind their machine guns. The interlude was over.

At the end of an hour, we saw the units come back, in step, as usual. Joyfully, I caught sight of my father.

"Several buildings have been flattened right out," he said, "but the warehouse hasn't suffered."

In the afternoon we went cheerfully to clear away the ruins.

A week later, on the way back from work, we noticed in the center of the camp, at the assembly place, a black gallows.

We were told that soup would not be distributed until after roll call. This took longer than usual. The orders were given in a sharper manner than on other days, and in the air there were strange undertones.

"Bare your heads!" yelled the head of the camp, suddenly.

Ten thousand caps were simultaneously removed.

"Cover your heads!"

Ten thousand caps went back onto their skulls, as quick as lightning.

The gate to the camp opened. An SS section appeared and surrounded us: one SS at every three paces. On the lookout towers the machine guns were trained on the assembly place.

"They fear trouble," whispered Juliek.

Two SS men had gone to the cells. They came back with the condemned man between them. He was a youth from Warsaw. He had three years of concentration camp life behind him. He was a strong, well-built boy, a giant in comparison with me.

His back to the gallows, his face turned toward his judge, who was the head of the camp, the boy was pale, but seemed more moved than afraid. His manacled hands did not tremble. His eyes gazed coldly at the hundreds of SS guards, the thousands of prisoners who surrounded him.

The head of the camp began to read his verdict, hammering out each phrase:

"In the name of Himmler . . . prisoner Number . . . stole during the alert. . . . According to the law . . . paragraph . . . prisoner Number . . . is condemned to death. May this be a warning and an example to all prisoners."

No one moved.

I could hear my heart beating. The thousands who had died daily at Auschwitz and at Birkenau in the crematory ovens no longer troubled me. But this one, leaning against his gallows— he overwhelmed me.

"Do you think this ceremony'll be over soon? I'm hungry. . . ." whispered Juliek.

At a sign from the head of the camp, the Lagerkapo advanced toward the condemned man. Two prisoners helped him in his task—for two plates of soup.

The Kapo wanted to bandage the victim's eyes, but he refused.

After a long moment of waiting, the executioner put the rope round his neck. He was on the point of motioning to his assistants to draw the chair away from the prisoner's feet, when the latter cried, in a calm, strong voice:

"Long live liberty! A curse upon Germany! A curse . . . ! A cur—"

The executioners had completed their task.

A command cleft the air like a sword.

"Bare your heads."

Ten thousand prisoners paid their last respects.

"Cover your heads!"

Then the whole camp, block after block, had to march past the hanged man and stare at the dimmed eyes, the lolling tongue of death. The Kapos and heads of each block forced everyone to look him full in the face.

After the march, we were given permission to return to the blocks for our meal.

I remember that I found the soup excellent that evening. . . .

I witnessed other hangings. I never saw a single one of the victims weep. For a long time those dried-up bodies had forgotten the bitter taste of tears.

Except once. The Oberkapo of the fifty-second cable unit was a Dutchman, a giant, well over six feet. Seven hundred prisoners worked under his orders, and they all loved him like a brother. No one had ever received a blow at his hands, nor an insult from his lips.

He had a young boy under him, a *pipel,* as they were called—a child with a refined and beautiful face, unheard of in this camp.

(At Buna, the *pipel* were loathed; they were often crueller than adults. I once saw one of thirteen beating his father because the latter had not made his bed properly. The old man was crying softly while the boy shouted: "If you don't stop crying at once I shan't bring you any more bread. Do you understand?" But the Dutchman's little servant was loved by all. He had the face of a sad angel.)

One day, the electric power station at Buna was blown up. The Gestapo, summoned to the spot, suspected sabotage. They found a trail. It eventually led to the Dutch Oberkapo. And there, after a search, they found an important stock of arms.

The Oberkapo was arrested immediately. He was tortured for a period of weeks, but in vain. He would not give a single name. He was transferred to Auschwitz. We never heard of him again.

But his little servant had been left behind in the camp in prison. Also put to torture, he too would not speak. Then the SS sentenced him to death, with two other prisoners who had been discovered with arms.

One day when we came back from work, we saw three gallows rearing up in the assembly place, three black crows. Roll call. SS all round us, machine guns trained: the traditional ceremony. Three victims in chains—and one of them, the little servant, the sad-eyed angel.

The SS seemed more preoccupied, more disturbed than usual. To hang a young boy in front of thousands of spectators was no light matter. The head of the camp read the verdict. All eyes were on the child. He was lividly pale, almost calm, biting his lips. The gallows threw its shadow over him.

This time the Lagerkapo refused to act as executioner. Three SS replaced him.

The three victims mounted together onto the chairs.

The three necks were placed at the same moment within the nooses.

"Long live liberty!" cried the two adults.

But the child was silent.

"Where is God? Where is He?" someone behind me asked.

At a sign from the head of the camp, the three chairs were tipped over.

Total silence throughout the camp. On the horizon, the sun was setting.

"Bare your heads!" yelled the head of the camp. His voice was raucous. We were weeping.

"Cover your heads!"

Then the march past began. The two adults were no longer alive. Their tongues hung swollen, blue-tinged. But the third rope was still moving; being so light, the child was still alive. . . .

For more than half an hour he stayed there, struggling between life and death, dying in slow agony under our eyes. And we had to look him full in the face. He was still alive when I passed in front of him. His tongue was still red, his eyes were not yet glazed.

Behind me, I heard the same man asking:

"Where is God now?"

And I heard a voice within me answer him:

"Where is He? Here He is—He is hanging here on this gallows. . . ."

That night the soup tasted of corpses.

5

THE summer was coming to an end. The Jewish year was nearly over.

On the eve of Rosh Hashanah, the last day of that accursed year, the whole camp was electric with the tension which was in all our hearts. In spite of everything, this day was different from any other. The last day of the year. The word "last" rang very strangely. What if it were indeed the last day?

They gave us our evening meal, a very thick soup, but no one touched it. We wanted to wait until after prayers. At the place of assembly, surrounded by the electrified barbed wire, thousands of silent Jews gathered, their faces stricken.

Night was falling. Other prisoners continued to crowd in, from every block, able suddenly to conquer time and space and submit both to their will.

"What are You, my God," I thought angrily, "compared to this afflicted crowd, proclaiming to You their faith, their anger, their revolt? What does Your greatness mean, Lord of the universe, in the face of all this weakness, this decomposition, and this decay? Why do You still trouble their sick minds, their crippled bodies?"

Ten thousand men had come to attend the solemn service, heads of the blocks, Kapos, functionaries of death.

"Bless the Eternal. . . ."

The voice of the officiant had just made itself heard. I thought at first it was the wind.

"Blessed be the Name of the Eternal!"

Thousands of voices repeated the benediction; thousands of men prostrated themselves like trees before a tempest.

"Blessed be the Name of the Eternal!"

Why, but why should I bless Him? In every fiber I rebelled. Because He had had thousands of children burned in His pits? Because He kept six crematories working night and day, on Sundays and feast days? Because in His great might He had created Auschwitz, Birkenau, Buna, and so many factories of death? How could I say to Him: "Blessed art Thou, Eternal, Master of the Universe, Who chose us from among the races to be tortured day and night, to see our fathers, our mothers, our brothers, end in the crematory? Praised be Thy Holy Name, Thou Who hast chosen us to be butchered on Thine altar?"

I heard the voice of the officiant rising up, powerful yet at the same time broken, amid the tears, sobs, the sighs of the whole congregation:

"All the earth and the Universe are God's!"

He kept stopping every moment, as though he did not have the strength to find the meaning beneath the words. The melody choked in his throat.

And I, mystic that I had been, I thought:

"Yes, man is very strong, greater than God. When You were deceived by Adam and Eve, You drove them out of Paradise. When Noah's generation displeased You, You brought down the Flood. When Sodom no longer found favor in Your eyes, You made the sky rain down fire and sulphur. But these men here, whom You have betrayed, whom You have allowed to be tortured, butchered, gassed, burned, what do they do? They pray before You! They praise Your name!"

"All creation bears witness to the Greatness of God!"

Once, New Year's Day had dominated my life. I knew that my sins grieved the Eternal; I implored his forgiveness. Once, I had believed profoundly that upon one solitary deed of mine, one solitary prayer, depended the salvation of the world.

This day I had ceased to plead. I was no longer capable of lamentation. On the contrary, I felt very strong. I was the accuser, God the accused. My eyes were open and I was alone— terribly alone in a world without God and without man. Without love or mercy. I had ceased to be anything but ashes, yet I felt myself to be stronger than the Almighty, to whom my life had been tied for so long. I stood amid that praying congregation, observing it like a stranger.

The service ended with the Kaddish. Everyone recited the Kaddish over his parents, over his children, over his brothers, and over himself.

We stayed for a long time at the assembly place. No one dared to drag himself away from this mirage. Then it was time to go to bed and slowly the prisoners made their way over to their blocks. I heard people wishing one another a Happy New Year!

I ran off to look for my father. And at the same time I was afraid of having to wish him a Happy New Year when I no longer believed in it.

He was standing near the wall, bowed down, his shoulders sagging as though beneath a heavy burden. I went up to him, took his hand and kissed it. A tear fell upon it. Whose was that

tear? Mine? His? I said nothing. Nor did he. We had never understood one another so clearly.

The sound of the bell jolted us back to reality. We must go to
bed. We came back from far away. I raised my eyes to look at my
father's face leaning over mine, to try to discover a smile or
something resembling one upon the aged, dried-up counte-
nance.. Nothing. Not the shadow of an expression. Beaten.

Yom Kippur. The Day of Atonement.

Should we fast? The question was hotly debated. To fast
would mean a surer, swifter death. We fasted here the whole
year round. The whole year was Yom Kippur. But others said
that we should fast simply because it was dangerous to do so.
We should show God that even here, in this enclosed hell, we
were capable of singing His praises.

I did not fast, mainly to please my father, who had forbidden
me to do so. But further, there was no longer any reason why I
should fast. I no longer accepted God's silence. As I swallowed
my bowl of soup, I saw in the gesture an act of rebellion and
protest against Him.

And I nibbled my crust of bread.

In the depths of my heart, I felt a great void.

The SS gave us a fine New Year's gift.

We had just come back from work. As soon as we had passed
through the door of the camp, we sensed something different in the
air. Roll call did not take so long as usual. The evening soup was
given out with great speed and swallowed down at once in anguish.

I was no longer in the same block as my father. I had been
transferred to another unit, the building one, where, twelve
hours a day, I had to drag heavy blocks of stone about. The
head of my new block was a German Jew, small of stature, with
piercing eyes. He told us that evening that no one would be allowed to go out after the evening soup. And soon a terrible word
was circulating—selection.

We knew what that meant. An SS man would examine us.
Whenever he found a weak one, a *musulman* as we called them,
he would write his number down: good for the crematory.

After soup, we gathered together between the beds. The veterans said:

"You're lucky to have been brought here so late. This camp is
paradise today, compared with what it was like two years ago.

Buna was a real hell then. There was no water, no blankets, less soup and bread. At night we slept almost naked, and it was below thirty degrees. The corpses were collected in hundreds every day. The work was hard. Today, this is a little paradise. The Kapos had orders to kill a certain number of prisoners every day. And every week—selection. A merciless selection. . . . Yes, you're lucky."

"Stop it! Be quiet!" I begged. "You can tell your stories tomorrow or on some other day."

They burst out laughing. They were not veterans for nothing.

"Are you scared? So were we scared. And there was plenty to be scared of in those days."

The old men stayed in their corner, dumb, motionless, haunted. Some were praying.

An hour's delay. In an hour, we should know the verdict—death or a reprieve.

And my father? Suddenly I remembered him. How would he pass the selection? He had aged so much. . . .

The head of our block had never been outside concentration camps since 1933. He had already been through all the slaughterhouses, all the factories of death. At about nine o'clock, he took up his position in our midst:

"Achtung!"

There was instant silence.

"Listen carefully to what I am going to say." (For the first time, I heard his voice quiver.) "In a few moments the selection will begin. You must get completely undressed. Then one by one you go before the SS doctors. I hope you will all succeed in getting through. But you must help your own chances. Before you go into the next room, move about in some way so that you give yourselves a little color. Don't walk slowly, run! Run as if the devil were after you! Don't look at the SS. Run, straight in front of you!"

He broke off for a moment, then added:

"And, the essential thing, don't be afraid!"

Here was a piece of advice we should have liked very much to be able to follow.

I got undressed, leaving my clothes on the bed. There was no danger of anyone stealing them this evening.

Tibi and Yossi, who had changed their unit at the same time as I had, came up to me and said:

"Let's keep together. We shall be stronger."

Yossi was murmuring something between his teeth. He must have been praying. I had never realized that Yossi was a believer. I had even always thought the reverse. Tibi was silent, very pale. All the prisoners in the block stood naked between the beds. This must be how one stands at the last judgment.

"They're coming!"

There were three SS officers standing round the notorious Dr. Mengele, who had received us at Birkenau. The head of the block, with an attempt at a smile, asked us:

"Ready?"

Yes, we were ready. So were the SS doctors. Dr. Mengele was holding a list in his hand: our numbers. He made a sign to the head of the block: "We can begin!" As if this were a game!

The first to go by were the "officials" of the block: *Stubenaelteste*, Kapos, foremen, all in perfect physical condition of course! Then came the ordinary prisoners' turn. Dr. Mengele took stock of them from head to foot. Every now and then, he wrote a number down. One single thought filled my mind: not to let my number be taken; not to show my left arm.

There were only Tibi and Yossi in front of me. They passed. I had time to notice that Mengele had not written their numbers down. Someone pushed me. It was my turn. I ran without looking back. My head was spinning: you're too thin, you're weak, you're too thin, you're good for the furnace. . . . The race seemed interminable. I thought I had been running for years. . . . You're too thin, you're too weak. . . . At last I had arrived exhausted. When I regained my breath, I questioned Yossi and Tibi:

"Was I written down?"

"No," said Yossi. He added, smiling: "In any case, he couldn't have written you down, you were running too fast. . . ."

I began to laugh. I was glad. I would have liked to kiss him. At that moment, what did the others matter! I hadn't been written down.

Those whose numbers had been noted stood apart, abandoned by the whole world. Some were weeping in silence.

The SS officers went away. The head of the block appeared, his face reflecting the general weariness.

"Everything went off all right. Don't worry. Nothing is going to happen to anyone. To anyone."

Again he tried to smile. A poor, emaciated, dried-up Jew questioned him avidly in a trembling voice:

"But . . . but, *Blockaelteste*, they did write me down!"

The head of the block let his anger break out. What! Did someone refuse to believe him!

"What's the matter now? Am I telling lies then? I tell you once and for all, nothing's going to happen to you! To anyone! You're wallowing in your own despair, you fool!"

The bell rang, a signal that the selection had been completed throughout the camp.

With all my might I began to run to Block 36. I met my father on the way. He came up to me:

"Well? So you passed?"

"Yes. And you?"

"Me too."

How we breathed again, now! My father had brought me a present—half a ration of bread obtained in exchange for a piece of rubber, found at the warehouse, which would do to sole a shoe.

The bell. Already we must separate, go to bed. Everything was regulated by the bell. It gave me orders, and I automatically obeyed them. I hated it. Whenever I dreamed of a better world, I could only imagine a universe with no bells.

Several days had elapsed. We no longer thought about the selection. We went to work as usual, loading heavy stones into railway wagons. Rations had become more meager: this was the only change.

We had risen before dawn, as on every day. We had received the black coffee, the ration of bread. We were about to set out for the yard as usual. The head of the block arrived, running.

"Silence for a moment. I have a list of numbers here. I'm going to read them to you. Those whose numbers I call won't be going to work this morning; they'll stay behind in the camp."

And, in a soft voice, he read out about ten numbers. We had understood. These were numbers chosen at the selection. Dr. Mengele had not forgotten.

The head of the block went toward his room. Ten prisoners surrounded him, hanging onto his clothes:

"Save us! You promised . . . ! We want to go to the yard. We're strong enough to work. We're good workers. We can . . . we will. . . ."

He tried to calm them, to reassure them about their fate, to explain to them that the fact that they were staying behind in the camp did not mean much, had no tragic significance.

"After all, I stay here myself every day," he added.

It was a somewhat feeble argument. He realized it, and without another word went and shut himself up in his room.

The bell had just rung.

"Form up!"

It scarcely mattered now that the work was hard. The essential thing was to be as far away as possible from the block, from the crucible of death, from the center of hell.

I saw my father running toward me. I became frightened all of a sudden.

"What's the matter?"

Out of breath, he could hardly open his mouth.

"Me, too . . . me, too . . . ! They told me to stay behind in the camp."

They had written down his number without his being aware of it.

"What will happen?" I asked in anguish.

But it was he who tried to reassure me.

"It isn't certain yet. There's still a chance of escape. They're going to do another selection today . . . a decisive selection."

I was silent.

He felt that his time was short. He spoke quickly. He would have liked to say so many things. His speech grew confused; his voice choked. He knew that I would have to go in a few moments. He would have to stay behind alone, so very alone.

"Look, take this knife," he said to me. "I don't need it any longer. It might be useful to you. And take this spoon as well. Don't sell them. Quickly! Go on. Take what I'm giving you!"

The inheritance.

"Don't talk like that, Father." (I felt that I would break into sobs.) "I don't want you to say that. Keep the spoon and knife. You need them as much as I do. We shall see each other again this evening, after work."

He looked at me with his tired eyes, veiled with despair. He went on:

"I'm asking this of you. . . . Take them. Do as I ask, my son. We have no time. . . . Do as your father asks."

Our Kapo yelled that we should start.

The unit set out toward the camp gate. Left, right! I bit my lips. My father had stayed by the block, leaning against the wall. Then he began to run, to catch up with us. Perhaps he had forgotten something he wanted to say to me. . . . But we were marching too quickly . . . Left, right!

We were already at the gate. They counted us, to the din of military music. We were outside.

The whole day, I wandered about as if sleepwalking. Now and then Tibi and Yossi would throw me a brotherly word. The Kapo,

Elie Wiesel

too, tried to reassure me. He had given me easier work today. I
felt sick at heart. How well they were treating me! Like an orphan!
I thought: even now, my father is still helping me.

I did not know myself what I wanted—for the day to pass
quickly or not. I was afraid of finding myself alone that night.
How good it would be to die here!

At last we began the return journey. How I longed for orders
to run!

The military march. The gate. The camp.

I ran to Block 36.

Were there still miracles on this earth? He was alive. He had
escaped the second selection. He had been able to prove that he
was still useful. . . . I gave him back his knife and spoon.

Akiba Drumer left us, a victim of the selection. Lately, he had
wandered among us, his eyes glazed, telling everyone of his
weakness: "I can't go on . . . It's all over. . . ." It was impossible
to raise his morale. He didn't listen to what we told him. He
could only repeat that all was over for him, that he could no
longer keep up the struggle, that he had no strength left, nor
faith. Suddenly his eyes would become blank, nothing but two
open wounds, two pits of terror.

He was not the only one to lose his faith during those selection days. I knew a rabbi from a little town in Poland, a bent old
man, whose lips were always trembling. He used to pray all the
time, in the block, in the yard, in the ranks. He would recite
whole pages of the Talmud from memory, argue with himself,
ask himself questions and answer himself. And one day he said
to me: "It's the end. God is no longer with us."

And, as though he had repented of having spoken such
words, so clipped, so cold, he added in his faint voice:

"I know. One has no right to say things like that. I know. Man
is too small, too humble and inconsiderable to seek to understand the mysterious ways of God. But what can I do? I'm not a
sage, one of the elect, nor a saint. I'm just an ordinary creature
of flesh and blood. I've got eyes, too, and I can see what they're
doing here. Where is the divine Mercy? Where is God? How can I
believe, how could anyone believe, in this merciful God?"

Poor Akiba Drumer, if he could have gone on believing in
God, if he could have seen a proof of God in this Calvary, he
would not have been taken by the selection. But as soon as he
felt the first cracks forming in his faith, he had lost his reason
for struggling and had begun to die.

When the selection came, he was condemned in advance, offering his own neck to the executioner. All he asked of us was:

"In three days I shall no longer be here. . . . Say the Kaddish for me."

We promised him. In three days' time, when we saw the smoke rising from the chimney, we would think of him. Ten of us would gather together and hold a special service. All his friends would say the Kaddish.

Then he went off toward the hospital, his step steadier, not looking back. An ambulance was waiting to take him to Birkenau.

These were terrible days. We received more blows than food; we were crushed with work. And three days after he had gone we forgot to say the Kaddish.

Winter had come. The days were short, and the nights had become almost unbearable. In the first hours of dawn, the icy wind cut us like a whip. We were given winter clothes—slightly thicker striped shirts. The veterans found in this a new source of derision.

"Now you'll really be getting a taste of the camp!"

We left for work as usual, our bodies frozen. The stones were so cold that it seemed as though our hands would be glued to them if we touched them. But you get used to anything.

On Christmas and New Year's Day, there was no work. We were allowed a slightly thicker soup.

Toward the middle of January, my right foot began to swell because of the cold. I was unable to put it on the ground. I went to have it examined. The doctor, a great Jewish doctor, a prisoner like ourselves, was quite definite: I must have an operation! If we waited, the toes—and perhaps the whole leg—would have to be amputated.

This was the last straw! But I had no choice. The doctor had decided on an operation, and there was no discussing it. I was even glad that it was he who had made the decision.

They put me into a bed with white sheets. I had forgotten that people slept in sheets.

The hospital was not bad at all. We were given good bread and thicker soup. No more bell. No more roll call. No more work. Now and then I was able to send a bit of bread to my father.

Near me lay a Hungarian Jew who had been struck down with dysentery—skin and bone, with dead eyes. I could only hear his voice; it was the sole indication that he was alive. Where did he get the strength to talk?

"You mustn't rejoice too soon, my boy. There's selection here too. More often than outside. Germany doesn't need sick Jews. Germany doesn't need me. When the next transport comes, you'll have a new neighbor. So listen to me, and take my advice: get out of the hospital before the next selection!"

These words which came from under the ground, from a faceless shape, filled me with terror. It was indeed true that the hospital was very small and that if new invalids arrived in the next few days, room would have to be found for them.

But perhaps my faceless neighbor, fearing that he would be among the first victims, simply wanted to drive me away, to free my bed in order to give himself a chance to survive. Perhaps he just wanted to frighten me. Yet, what if he were telling the truth? I decided to await events.

The doctor came to tell me that the operation would be the next day.

"Don't be afraid," he added. "Everything will be all right."

At ten o'clock in the morning, they took me into the operating room. "My" doctor was there. I took comfort from this. I felt that nothing serious could happen while he was there. There was balm in every word he spoke, and every glance he gave me held a message of hope.

"It will hurt you a bit," he said, "but that will pass. Grit your teeth."

The operation lasted an hour. They had not put me to sleep. I kept my eyes fixed upon my doctor. Then I felt myself go under. . . .

When I came round, opening my eyes, I could see nothing at first but a great whiteness, my sheets; then I noticed the face of my doctor, bending over me:

"Everything went off well. You're brave, my boy. Now you're going to stay here for two weeks, rest comfortably, and it will be over. You'll eat well, and relax your body and your nerves."

I could only follow the movements of his lips. I scarcely understood what he was saying, but the murmur of his voice did me good. Suddenly a cold sweat broke out on my forehead. I could not feel my leg! Had they amputated it?

"Doctor," I stammered. "Doctor . . . ?"

"What's the matter, son?"

I lacked the courage to ask him the question.

"Doctor, I'm thirsty . . ."

He had water brought to me. He was smiling. He was getting ready to go and visit the other patients.

"Doctor?"

"What?"

"Shall I still be able to use my leg?"

He was no longer smiling. I was very frightened. He said:

"Do you trust me, my boy?"

"I trust you absolutely, Doctor."

"Well then, listen to me. You'll be completely recovered in a fortnight. You'll be able to walk like anyone else. The sole of your foot was all full of puss. We just had to open the swelling. You haven't had your leg amputated. You'll see. In a fortnight's time you'll be walking about like everyone else."

I had only a fortnight to wait.

Two days after my operation, there was a rumor going round the camp that the front had suddenly drawn nearer. The Red Army, they said, was advancing on Buna; it was only a matter of hours now.

We were already accustomed to rumors of this kind. It was not the first time a false prophet had foretold to us peace-on-earth, negotiations-with-the-Red-Cross-for-our-release, or other false rumors. . . . And often we believed them. It was an injection of morphine.

But this time these prophecies seemed more solid. During these last few nights, we had heard the guns in the distance.

My neighbor, the faceless one, said:

"Don't let yourself be fooled with illusions. Hitler has made it very clear that he will annihilate all the Jews before the clock strikes twelve, before they can hear the last stroke."

I burst out:

"What does it matter to you? Do we have to regard Hitler as a prophet?"

His glazed, faded eyes looked at me. At last he said in a weary voice:

"I've got more faith in Hitler than in anyone else. He's the only one who's kept his promises, all his promises, to the Jewish people."

At four o'clock on the afternoon of the same day, as usual the bell summoned all the heads of the blocks to go and report.

They came back shattered. They could only just open their lips enough to say the word: evacuation. The camp was to be emptied, and we were to be sent farther back. Where to? To somewhere right in the depths of Germany, to other camps; there was no shortage of them.

"When?"

"Tomorrow evening."

"Perhaps the Russians will arrive first."

"Perhaps."

We knew perfectly well that they would not.

The camp had become a hive. People ran about, shouting at one another. In all the blocks, preparations for the journey were going on. I had forgotten about my bad foot. A doctor came into the room and announced:

"Tomorrow, immediately after nightfall, the camp will set out. Block after block. Patients will stay in the infirmary. They will not be evacuated."

This news made us think. Were the SS going to leave hundreds of prisoners to strut about in the hospital blocks, waiting for their liberators? Were they going to let the Jews hear the twelfth stroke sound? Obviously not.

"All the invalids will be summarily killed," said the faceless one. "And sent to the crematory in a final batch."

"The camp is certain to be mined," said another. "The moment the evacuation's over, it'll blow up."

As for me, I was not thinking about death, but I did not want to be separated from my father. We had already suffered so much, borne so much together; this was not the time to be separated.

I ran outside to look for him. The snow was thick, and the windows of the blocks were veiled with frost. One shoe in my hand, because it would not go onto my right foot, I ran on, feeling neither pain nor cold.

"What shall we do?"

My father did not answer.

"What shall we do, father?"

He was lost in thought. The choice was in our hands. For once we could decide our fate for ourselves. We could both stay in the hospital, where I could, thanks to my doctor, get him entered as a patient or a nurse. Or else we could follow the others.

"Well, what shall we do, father?"

He was silent.

"Let's be evacuated with the others," I said to him.

He did not answer. He looked at my foot.

"Do you think you can walk?"

"Yes, I think so."

"Let's hope that we shan't regret it, Eliezer."

I learned after the war the fate of those who had stayed behind in the hospital. They were quite simply liberated by the Russians two days after the evacuation.

I did not go back to the hospital again. I returned to my block. My wound was open and bleeding; the snow had grown red where I had trodden.

The head of the block gave out double rations of bread and margarine, for the journey. We could take as many shirts and other clothes as we liked from the store.

It was cold. We got into bed.

The last night in Buna. Yet another last night. The last night at home, the last night in the ghetto, the last night in the train, and, now, the last night in Buna. How much longer were our lives to be dragged out from one "last night" to another?

I did not sleep at all. Through the frosted panes bursts of red light could be seen. Cannon shots split the nighttime silence. How close the Russians were! Between them and us—one night, our last night. There was whispering from one bed to another: with luck the Russians would be here before the evacuation. Hope revived again.

Someone shouted:

"Try and sleep. Gather your strength for the journey."

This reminded me of my mother's last words of advice in the ghetto.

But I could not sleep. My foot felt as if it were burning.

In the morning, the face of the camp had changed. Prisoners appeared in strange outfits: it was like a masquerade. Everyone had put on several garments, one on top of the other, in order to keep out the cold. Poor mountebanks, wider than they were tall, more dead than alive; poor clowns, their ghostlike faces emerging from piles of prison clothes! Buffoons!

I tried to find a shoe that was too large. In vain. I tore up a blanket and wrapped my wounded foot in it. Then I went wandering through the camp, looking for a little more bread and a few potatoes.

Some said we were being taken to Czechoslovakia. No, to Gros-Rosen. No, to Gleiwitz. No, to. . . .

Two o'clock in the afternoon. The snow was still coming down thickly.

The time was passing quickly now. Dusk had fallen. The day was disappearing in a monochrome of gray.

The head of the block suddenly remembered that he had forgotten to clean out the block. He ordered four prisoners to wash the wooden floor. . . . An hour before leaving the camp! Why? For whom?

"For the liberating army," he cried. "So that they'll realize there were men living here and not pigs."

Were we men then? The block was cleaned from top to bottom, washed in every corner.

At six o'clock the bell rang. The death knell. The burial. The procession was about to begin its march.

"Form up! Quickly!"

In a few moments we were all in rows, by blocks. Night had fallen. Everything was in order, according to the prearranged plan.

The searchlights came on. Hundreds of armed SS men rose up out of the darkness, accompanied by sheepdogs. The snow never ceased.

The gates of the camp opened. It seemed that an even darker night was waiting for us on the other side.

The first blocks began to march. We waited. We had to wait for the departure of the fifty-six blocks who came before us. It was very cold. In my pocket I had two pieces of bread. With how much pleasure could I have eaten them! But I was not allowed to. Not yet.

Our turn was coming: Block 53 . . . Block 55 . . .

Block 57, forward march!

It snowed relentlessly.

6

AN icy wind blew in violent gusts. But we marched without faltering.

The SS made us increase our pace. "Faster, you swine, you filthy sons of bitches!" Why not? The movement warmed us up a little. The blood flowed more easily in our veins. One felt oneself reviving. . . .

"Faster, you filthy sons of bitches!" We were no longer marching; we were running. Like automatons. The SS were running too, their weapons in their hands. We looked as though we were fleeing before them.

Pitch darkness. Every now and then, an explosion in the night. They had orders to fire on any who could not keep up. Their fingers on the triggers, they did not deprive themselves of this pleasure. If one of us stopped for a second, a sharp shot finished off another filthy son of a bitch.

I was putting one foot in front of the other mechanically. I was dragging with me this skeletal body which weighed so much. If only I could have got rid of it! In spite of my efforts not to think about it, I could feel myself as two entities—my body and me. I hated it.

I repeated to myself: "Don't think. Don't stop. Run."

Near me, men were collapsing in the dirty snow. Shots.

At my side marched a young Polish lad called Zalman. He had been working in the electrical warehouse at Buna. They had laughed at him because he was always praying or meditating on some problem of the Talmud. It was his way of escaping from reality, of not feeling the blows. . . .

He was suddenly seized with cramp in the stomach. "I've got stomach ache," he whispered to me. He could not go on. He had to stop for a moment. I begged him:

"Wait a bit, Zalman. We shall all be stopping soon. We're not going to run like this till the end of the world."

But as he ran he began to undo his buttons, crying:

"I can't go on any longer. My stomach's bursting. . . ."

"Make an effort, Zalman. . . . Try. . . ."

"I can't. . . ." he groaned.

His trousers lowered, he let himself sink down.

That is the last picture I have of him. I do not think it can have been the SS who finished him, because no one had noticed. He must have been trampled to death beneath the feet of the thousands of men who followed us.

I quickly forgot him. I began to think of myself again. Because of my painful foot, a shudder went through me at each step. "A few more yards." I thought. "A few more yards, and that will be the end. I shall fall. A spurt of red flame. A shot." Death wrapped itself around me till I was stifled. It stuck to me. I felt that I could touch it. The idea of dying, of no longer being, began to fascinate me. Not to exist any longer. Not to feel the horrible pains in my foot. Not to feel anything, neither weariness, nor cold, nor anything. To break the ranks, to let oneself slide to the edge of the road. . . .

My father's presence was the only thing that stopped me. . . . He was running at my side, out of breath, at the end of his strength, at his wit's end. I had no right to let myself die. What would he do without me? I was his only support.

These thoughts had taken up a brief space of time, during which I had gone on running without feeling my throbbing foot, without realizing that I was running, without being conscious that I owned a body galloping there on the road in the midst of so many thousands of others.

When I came to myself again, I tried to slacken the pace. But there was no way. A great tidal wave of men came rolling onward and would have crushed me like an ant.

I was simply walking in my sleep. I managed to close my eyes and to run like that while asleep. Now and then, someone would push me violently from behind, and I would wake up. The other would shout: "Run faster. If you don't want to go on, let other people come past." All I had to do was to close my eyes for a second to see a whole world passing by, to dream a whole lifetime.

An endless road. Letting oneself be pushed by the mob; letting oneself be dragged along by a blind destiny. When the SS became tired, they were changed. But no one changed us. Our limbs numb with cold despite the running, our throats parched, famished, breathless, on we went.

We were masters of nature, masters of the world. We had forgotten everything—death, fatigue, our natural needs. Stronger than cold or hunger, stronger than the shots and the desire to die, condemned and wandering, mere numbers, we were the only men on earth.

At last, the morning star appeared in the gray sky. A trail of indeterminate light showed on the horizon. We were exhausted. We were without strength, without illusions.

The commandant announced that we had already covered forty-two miles since we left. It was a long time since we had passed beyond the limits of fatigue. Our legs were moving mechanically, in spite of us, without us.

We went through a deserted village. Not a living soul. Not the bark of a dog. Houses with gaping windows. A few slipped out of the ranks to try and hide in some deserted building.

Still one hour's marching more, and at last came the order to rest.

We sank down as one man in the snow. My father shook me.

"Not here. . . . Get up. . . . A little farther on. There's a shed over there . . . come on."

I had neither the will nor the strength to get up. Nevertheless I obeyed. It was not a shed, but a brick factory with a caved-in roof, broken windows, walls filthy with soot. It was not easy to get in. Hundreds of prisoners were crowding at the door.

We at last succeeded in getting inside. There too the snow was thick. I let myself sink down. It was only then that I really felt my weariness. The snow was like a carpet, very gentle, very warm. I fell asleep.

I do not know how long I slept. A few moments or an hour. When I woke up, a frozen hand was patting my cheeks. I forced myself to open my eyes. It was my father.

How old he had grown since the night before! His body was completely twisted, shriveled up into itself. His eyes were petrified, his lips withered, decayed. Everything about him bore witness to extreme exhaustion. His voice was damp with tears and snow:

"Don't let yourself be overcome by sleep, Eliezer. It's dangerous to fall asleep in the snow. You might sleep for good. Come on, come on. Get up."

Get up? How could I? How could I get myself out of this fluffy bed? I could hear what my father said, but it seemed empty of meaning, as though he had told me to lift up the whole building in my arms. . . .

"Come on, son, come on. . . ."

I got up, gritting my teeth. Supporting me with his arm, he led me outside. It was far from easy. It was as difficult to go out as to get in. Under our feet were men crushed, trampled underfoot, dying. No one paid any attention.

We were outside. The icy wind stung my face. I bit my lips continually to prevent them from freezing. Around me everything was dancing a dance of death. It made my head reel. I was walking in a cemetery, among stiffened corpses, logs of wood. Not a cry of distress, not a groan, nothing but a mass agony, in silence. No one asked anyone else for help. You died because you had to die. There was no fuss.

In every stiffened corpse I saw myself. And soon I should not even see them; I should be one of them—a matter of hours.

"Come on, father, let's go back to the shed. . . ."

He did not answer. He was not looking at the dead.

"Come on, father, it's better over there. We can lie down a bit, one after the other. I'll watch over you, and then you can watch over me. We won't let each other fall asleep. We'll look after each other."

He agreed. Trampling over living bodies and corpses, we managed to re-enter the shed. Here we let ourselves sink down.

"Don't be afraid, son. Sleep—you can sleep. I'll look after you myself."

"No, you first, father. Go to sleep."

He refused. I lay down and tried to force myself to sleep, to doze a little, but in vain. God knows what I would not have given for a few moments of sleep. But, deep down, I felt that to sleep would mean to die. And something within me revolted against this death. All round me death was moving in, silently, without violence. It would seize upon some sleeping being, enter into him, and consume him bit by bit. Next to me there was someone trying to wake up his neighbor, his brother, perhaps, or a friend. In vain. Discouraged in the attempt, the man lay down in his turn, next to the corpse, and slept too. Who was there to wake him up? Stretching out an arm, I touched him:

"Wake up. You mustn't sleep here. . . ."

He half opened his eyes.

"No advice," he said in a faint voice. "I'm tired. Leave me alone. Leave me."

My father, too, was gently dozing. I could not see his eyes. His cap had fallen over his face.

"Wake up," I whispered in his ear.

He started up. He sat up and looked round him, bewildered, stupefied—a bereaved stare. He stared all round him in a circle as though he had suddenly decided to draw up an inventory of his universe, to find out exactly where he was, in what place, and why. Then he smiled.

I shall always remember that smile. From which world did it come?

The snow continued to fall in thick flakes over the corpses.

The door of the shed opened. An old man appeared, his moustache covered with frost, his lips blue with cold. It was Rabbi Eliahou, the rabbi of a small Polish community. He was a very good man, well loved by everyone in the camp, even by the Kapos and the heads of the blocks. Despite the trials and privations, his face still shone with his inner purity. He was the only rabbi who was always addressed as "Rabbi" at Buna. He was like one of the old prophets, always in the midst of his people to comfort them. And, strangely, his words of comfort never provoked rebellion; they really brought peace.

He came into the shed and his eyes, brighter than ever, seemed to be looking for someone:

"Perhaps someone has seen my son somewhere?"

He had lost his son in the crowd. He had looked in vain among the dying. Then he had scratched up the snow to find his corpse. Without result.

For three years they had stuck together. Always near each other, for suffering, for blows, for the ration of bread, for prayer. Three years, from camp to camp, from selection to selection. And now—when the end seemed near—fate had separated them. Finding himself near me, Rabbi Eliahou whispered:

"It happened on the road. We lost sight of one another during the journey. I had stayed a little to the rear of the column. I hadn't any strength left for running. And my son didn't notice. That's all I know. Where has he disappeared? Where can I find him? Perhaps you've seen him somewhere?"

"No, Rabbi Eliahou, I haven't seen him."

He left then as he had come: like a wind-swept shadow.

He had already passed through the door when I suddenly remembered seeing his son running by my side. I had forgotten that, and I didn't tell Rabbi Eliahou!

Then I remembered something else: his son had seen him losing ground, limping, staggering back to the rear of the column. He had seen him. And he had continued to run on in front, letting the distance between them grow greater.

A terrible thought loomed up in my mind: he had wanted to get rid of his father! He had felt that his father was growing weak, he had believed that the end was near and had sought this separation in order to get rid of the burden, to free himself from an encumbrance which could lessen his own chances of survival.

I had done well to forget that. And I was glad that Rabbi Eliahou should continue to look for his beloved son.

And, in spite of myself, a prayer rose in my heart, to that God in whom I no longer believed.

My God, Lord of the Universe, give me strength never to do what Rabbi Eliahou's son has done.

Shouts rose outside in the yard, where darkness had fallen. The SS ordered the ranks to form up.

The march began again. The dead stayed in the yard under the snow, like faithful guards assassinated, without burial. No one had said the prayer for the dead over them. Sons abandoned their fathers' remains without a tear.

On the way it snowed, snowed, snowed endlessly. We were marching more slowly. The guards themselves seemed tired. My wounded foot no longer hurt me. It must have been completely frozen. The foot was lost to me. It had detached itself from my body like the wheel of a car. Too bad. I should have to resign myself; I could live with only one leg. The main thing was not to think about it. Above all, not at this moment. Leave thoughts for later.

Our march had lost all semblance of discipline. We went as we wanted, as we could. We heard no more shots. Our guards must have been tired.

But death scarcely needed any help from them. The cold was conscientiously doing its work. At every step someone fell and suffered no more.

From time to time, SS officers on motorcycles would go down the length of the column to try and shake us out of our growing apathy:

"Keep going! We are getting there!"

"Courage! Only a few more hours!"

"We're reaching Gleiwitz."

These words of encouragement, even though they came from the mouths of our assassins, did us a great deal of good. No one wanted to give up now, just before the end, so near to the goal. Our eyes searched the horizon for the barbed wire of Gleiwitz. Our only desire was to reach it as quickly as possible.

The night had now set in. The snow had ceased to fall. We walked for several more hours before arriving.

We did not notice the camp until we were just in front of the gate.

Some Kapos rapidly installed us in the barracks. We pushed and jostled one another as if this were the supreme refuge, the gateway to life. We walked over pain-racked bodies. We trod on wounded faces. No cries. A few groans. My father and I were ourselves thrown to the ground by this rolling tide. Beneath our feet someone let out a rattling cry:

"You're crushing me . . . mercy!"

A voice that was not unknown to me.

"You're crushing me . . . mercy! mercy!"

The same faint voice, the same rattle, heard somewhere before. That voice had spoken to me one day. Where? When? Years ago? No, it could only have been at the camp.

"Mercy!"

I felt that I was crushing him. I was stopping his breath. I wanted to get up. I struggled to disengage myself, so that he could breathe. But I was crushed myself beneath the weight of other bodies. I could hardly breathe. I dug my nails into unknown faces. I was biting all round me, in order to get air. No one cried out.

Suddenly I remembered. Juliek! The boy from Warsaw who played the violin in the band at Buna. . . .

"Juliek, is it you?"

"Eliezer . . . the twenty-five strokes of the whip. Yes . . . I remember."

He was silent. A long moment elapsed.

"Juliek! Can you hear me, Juliek?"

"Yes . . . ," he said, in a feeble voice. "What do you want?"

He was not dead.

"How do you feel, Juliek?" I asked, less to know the answer than to hear that he could speak, that he was alive.

"All right, Eliezer. . . . I'm getting on all right . . . hardly any air . . . worn out. My feet are swollen. It's good to rest, but my violin. . . ."

I thought he had gone out of his mind. What use was the violin here?

"What, your violin?"

He gasped.

"I'm afraid . . . I'm afraid . . . that they'll break my violin. . . . I've brought it with me."

I could not answer him. Someone was lying full length on top of me, covering my face. I was unable to breathe, through either mouth or nose. Sweat beaded my brow, ran down my spine. This was the end—the end of the road. A silent death, suffocation. No way of crying out, of calling for help.

I tried to get rid of my invisible assassin. My whole will to live was centered in my nails. I scratched. I battled for a mouthful of air. I tore at decaying flesh which did not respond. I could not free myself from this mass weighing down my chest. Was it a dead man I was struggling against? Who knows?

I shall never know. All I can say is that I won. I succeeded in digging a hole through this wall of dying people, a little hole through which I could drink in a small quantity of air.

"Father, how are you?" I asked, as soon as I could utter a word.

I knew he could not be far from me.

"Well!" answered a distant voice, which seemed to come from another world. I tried to sleep.

He tried to sleep. Was he right or wrong? Could one sleep here? Was it not dangerous to allow your vigilance to fail, even for a moment, when at any minute death could pounce upon you?

I was thinking of this when I heard the sound of a violin. The sound of a violin, in this dark shed, where the dead were heaped on the living. What madman could be playing the violin here, at the brink of his own grave? Or was it really an hallucination?

It must have been Juliek.

He played a fragment from Beethoven's concerto. I had never heard sounds so pure. In such a silence.

How had he managed to free himself? To draw his body from under mine without my being aware of it?

It was pitch dark. I could hear only the violin, and it was as though Juliek's soul were the bow. He was playing his life. The whole of his life was gliding on the strings—his lost hopes, his charred past, his extinguished future. He played as he would never play again.

I shall never forget Juliek. How could I forget that concert, given to an audience of dying and dead men! To this day, whenever I hear Beethoven played my eyes close and out of the dark rises the sad, pale face of my Polish friend, as he said farewell on his violin to an audience of dying men.

I do not know for how long he played. I was overcome by sleep. When I awoke, in the daylight, I could see Juliek, opposite me, slumped over, dead. Near him lay his violin, smashed, trampled, a strange overwhelming little corpse.

We stayed at Gleiwitz for three days. Three days without food or drink. We were not allowed to leave the barracks. SS men guarded the door.

I was hungry and thirsty. I must have been very dirty and exhausted, to judge from the appearance of the others. The bread we had brought from Buna had long since been devoured. And who knew when we would be given another ration?

The front was following us. We could hear new gun shots again, very close. But we had neither the strength nor the courage to believe that the Nazis would not have time to evacuate us, and that the Russians would soon be here.

We heard that we were going to be deported into the center of Germany.

On the third day, at dawn, we were driven out of the barracks. We all threw blankets over our shoulders, like prayer
shawls. We were directed toward a gate which divided the camp
into two. A group of SS officers were standing there. A rumor
ran through our ranks—a selection!

The SS officers did the selecting. The weak, to the left; those
who could walk well, to the right.

My father was sent to the left. I ran after him. An SS officer
shouted at my back:

"Come back here!"

I slipped in among the others. Several SS rushed to bring me
back, creating such confusion that many of the people from the
left were able to come back to the right—and among them, my father and myself. However, there were some shots and some dead.

We were all made to leave the camp. After half an hour's
marching we arrived right in the middle of a field divided by
rails. We had to wait for the train to arrive.

The snow fell thickly. We were forbidden to sit down or even
to move.

The snow began to form a thick layer over our blankets. They
brought us bread—the usual ration. We threw ourselves upon
it. Someone had the idea of appeasing his thirst by eating the
snow. Soon the others were imitating him. As we were not
allowed to bend down, everyone took out his spoon and ate the
accumulated snow off his neighbor's back. A mouthful of bread
and a spoonful of snow. The SS who were watching laughed at
this spectacle.

Hours went by. Our eyes grew weary of scouring the horizon
for the liberating train. It did not arrive until much later in the
evening. An infinitely long train, composed of cattle wagons,
with no roofs. The SS pushed us in, a hundred to a carriage, we
were so thin! Our embarkation completed, the convoy set out.

7

PRESSED up against the others in an effort to keep out the cold, head empty and heavy at the same time, brain a whirlpool of decaying memories. Indifference deadened the spirit. Here or elsewhere—what difference did it make? To die today or tomorrow, or later? The night was long and never ending.

When at last a gray glimmer of light appeared on the horizon, it revealed a tangle of human shapes, heads sunk upon shoulders, crouched, piled one on top of the other, like a field of dust-covered tombstones in the first light of the dawn. I tried to distinguish those who were still alive from those who had gone. But there was no difference. My gaze was held for a long time by one who lay with his eyes open, staring into the void. His livid face was covered with a layer of frost and snow.

My father was huddled near me, wrapped in his blanket, his shoulders covered with snow. And was he dead, too? I called him. No answer. I would have cried out if I could have done so. He did not move.

My mind was invaded suddenly by this realization—there was no more reason to live, no more reason to struggle.

The train stopped in the middle of a deserted field. The suddenness of the halt woke some of those who were asleep. They straightened themselves up, throwing startled looks around them.

Outside, the SS went by, shouting:

"Throw out all the dead! All corpses outside!"

The living rejoiced. There would be more room. Volunteers set to work. They felt those who were still crouching.

"Here's one! Take him!"

They undressed him, the survivors avidly sharing out his clothes, then two "gravediggers" took him, one by the head and one by the feet, and threw him out of the wagon like a sack of flour.

From all directions came cries:

"Come on! Here's one! This man next to me. He doesn't move."

I woke from my apathy just at the moment when two men came up to my father. I threw myself on top of his body. He was cold. I slapped him. I rubbed his hands, crying:

"Father! Father! Wake up. They're trying to throw you out of the carriage. . . ."

His body remained inert.

The two gravediggers seized me by the collar.

"Leave him. You can see perfectly well that he's dead."

"No!" I cried. "He isn't dead! Not yet!"

I set to work to slap him as hard as I could. After a moment my father's eyelids moved slightly over his glazed eyes. He was breathing weakly.

"You see," I cried.

The two men moved away.

Twenty bodies were thrown out of our wagon. Then the train resumed its journey, leaving behind it a few hundred naked dead, deprived of burial, in the deep snow of a field in Poland.

We were given no food. We lived on snow; it took the place of bread. The days were like nights, and the nights left the dregs of their darkness in our souls. The train was traveling slowly, often stopping for several hours and then setting off again. It never ceased snowing. All through these days and nights we stayed crouching, one on top of the other, never speaking a word. We were no more than frozen bodies. Our eyes closed, we waited merely for the next stop, so that we could unload our dead.

Ten days, ten nights of traveling. Sometimes we would pass through German townships. Very early in the morning, usually. The workmen were going to work. They stopped and stared after us, but otherwise showed no surprise.

One day when we had stopped, a workman took a piece of bread out of his bag and threw it into a wagon. There was a stampede. Dozens of starving men fought each other to the death for a few crumbs. The German workmen took a lively interest in this spectacle.

Some years later, I watched the same kind of scene at Aden. The passengers on our boat were amusing themselves by throwing coins to the "natives," who were diving in to get them. An attractive, aristocratic Parisienne was deriving special pleasure from the game. I suddenly noticed that two children were engaged in a death struggle, trying to strangle each other. I turned to the lady.

"Please," I begged, "don't throw any more money in!"

"Why not?" she said. "I like to give charity. . . ."

In the wagon where the bread had fallen, a real battle had broken out. Men threw themselves on top of each other, stamping on each other, tearing at each other, biting each other. Wild beasts of prey, with animal hatred in their eyes; an extraordinary vitality had seized them, sharpening their teeth and nails.

A crowd of workmen and curious spectators had collected along the train. They had probably never seen a train with such a cargo. Soon, nearly everywhere, pieces of bread were being dropped into the wagons. The audience stared at these skeletons of men, fighting one another to the death for a mouthful.

A piece fell into our wagon. I decided that I would not move. Anyway, I knew that I would never have the strength to fight with a dozen savage men! Not far away I noticed an old man dragging himself along on all fours. He was trying to disengage himself from the struggle. He held one hand to his heart. I thought at first he had received a blow in the chest. Then I understood; he had a bit of bread under his shirt. With remarkable speed he drew it out and put it to his mouth. His eyes gleamed; a smile, like a grimace, lit up his dead face. And was immediately extinguished. A shadow had just loomed up near him. The shadow threw itself upon him. Felled to the ground, stunned with blows, the old man cried:

"Meir. Meir, my boy! Don't you recognize me? I'm your father . . . you're hurting me . . . you're killing your father! I've got some bread . . . for you too . . . for you too. . . ."

He collapsed. His fist was still clenched around a small piece. He tried to carry it to his mouth. But the other one threw himself upon him and snatched it. The old man again whispered something, let out a rattle, and died amid the general indifference. His son searched him, took the bread, and began to devour it. He was not able to get very far. Two men had seen and hurled themselves upon him. Others joined in. When they withdrew, next to me were two corpses, side by side, the father and the son.

I was fifteen years old.

In our wagon, there was a friend of my father's called Meir Katz. He had worked as a gardener at Buna and used to bring us a few green vegetables occasionally. Being less undernourished than the rest of us, he had stood up to imprisonment better. Because he was relatively more vigorous, he had been put in charge of the wagon.

On the third night of our journey I woke up suddenly and felt two hands on my throat, trying to strangle me. I just had the time to shout, "Father!"

Nothing but this word. I felt myself suffocating. But my father had woken up and seized my attacker. Too weak to overcome him, he had the idea of calling Meir Katz.

"Come here! Come quickly! There's someone strangling my son."

A few moments later I was free. I still do not know why the man wanted to strangle me.

After a few days, Meir Katz spoke to my father:

"Chlomo, I'm getting weak. I'm losing my strength. I can't hold on. . . ."

"Don't let yourself go under," my father said, trying to encourage him. "You must resist. Don't lose faith in yourself."

But Meir Katz groaned heavily in reply.

"I can't go on any longer, Chlomo! What can I do? I can't carry on. . . ."

My father took his arm. And Meir Katz, the strong man, the most robust of us all, wept. His son had been taken from him at the time of the first selection, but it was now that he wept. It was now that he cracked up. He was finished, at the end of his tether.

On the last day of our journey a terrible wind arose; it snowed without ceasing. We felt that the end was near—the real end. We could never hold out in this icy wind, in these gusts.

Someone got up and shouted:

"We mustn't stay sitting down at a time like this. We shall freeze to death! Let's all get up and move a bit. . . ."

We all got up. We held our damp blankets more tightly around us. And we forced ourselves to move a few steps, to turn around where we were.

Suddenly a cry rose up from the wagon, the cry of a wounded animal. Someone had just died.

Others, feeling that they too were about to die, imitated his cry. And their cries seemed to come from beyond the grave. Soon everyone was crying out. Wailing, groaning, cries of distress hurled into the wind and the snow.

The contagion spread to the other carriages. Hundreds of cries rose up simultaneously. Not knowing against whom we cried. Not knowing why. The death rattle of a whole convoy who felt the end upon them. We were all going to die here. All limits had been passed. No one had any strength left. And again the night would be long.

Meir Katz groaned:

"Why don't they shoot us all right away?"

That same evening, we reached our destination.

It was late at night. The guards came to unload us. The dead were abandoned in the train. Only those who could still stand were able to get out.

Meir Katz stayed in the train. The last day had been the most murderous. A hundred of us had got into the wagon. A dozen of us got out—among them, my father and I.

We had arrived at Buchenwald.

8

AT the gate of the camp, SS officers were waiting for us. They counted us. Then we were directed to the assembly place. Orders were given us through loudspeakers:

"Form fives!" "Form groups of a hundred!" "Five paces forward!"

I held onto my father's hand—the old, familiar fear: not to lose him.

Right next to us the high chimney of the crematory oven rose up. It no longer made any impression on us. It scarcely attracted our attention.

An established inmate of Buchenwald told us that we should have a shower and then we could go into the blocks. The idea of having a hot bath fascinated me. My father was silent. He was breathing heavily beside me.

"Father," I said. "Only another moment more. Soon we can lie down—in a bed. You can rest. . . ."

He did not answer. I was so exhausted myself that his silence left me indifferent. My only wish was to take a bath as quickly as possible and lie down in a bed.

But it was not easy to reach the showers. Hundreds of prisoners were crowding there. The guards were unable to keep any order. They struck out right and left with no apparent result. Others, without the strength to push or even to stand up, had sat down in the snow. My father wanted to do the same. He groaned.

"I can't go on. . . . This is the end. . . . I'm going to die here. . . ."

He dragged me toward a hillock of snow from which emerged human shapes and ragged pieces of blanket.

"Leave me," he said to me. "I can't go on. . . . Have mercy on me. . . . I'll wait here until we can get into the baths. . . . You can come and find me."

I could have wept with rage. Having lived through so much, suffered so much, could I leave my father to die now? Now, when we could have a good hot bath and lie down?

"Father!" I screamed. "Father! Get up from here! Immediately! You're killing yourself. . . ."

I seized him by the arm. He continued to groan.

"Don't shout, son. . . . Take pity on your old father. . . . Leave me to rest here. . . . Just for a bit, I'm so tired . . . at the end of my strength. . . ."

He had become like a child, weak, timid, vulnerable.

"Father," I said. "You can't stay here."

I showed him the corpses all around him; they too had wanted to rest here.

"I can see them, son. I can see them all right. Let them sleep. It's so long since they closed their eyes. . . . They are exhausted . . . exhausted. . . ."

His voice was tender.

I yelled against the wind:

"They'll never wake again! Never! Don't you understand?"

For a long time this argument went on. I felt that I was not arguing with him, but with death itself, with the death that he had already chosen.

The sirens began to wail. An alert. The lights went out throughout the camp. The guards drove us toward the blocks. In a flash, there was no one left on the assembly place. We were only too glad not to have had to stay outside longer in the icy wind. We let ourselves sink down onto the planks. The beds were in several tiers. The cauldrons of soup at the entrance attracted no one. To sleep, that was all that mattered.

It was daytime when I awoke. And then I remembered that I had a father. Since the alert, I had followed the crowd without troubling about him. I had known that he was at the end, on the brink of death, and yet I had abandoned him.

I went to look for him.

But at the same moment this thought came into my mind: "Don't let me find him! If only I could get rid of this dead weight, so that I could use all my strength to struggle for my own survival, and only worry about myself." Immediately I felt ashamed of myself, ashamed forever.

I walked for hours without finding him. Then I came to the block where they were giving out black "coffee." The men were lining up and fighting.

A plaintive, beseeching voice caught me in the spine:

"Eliezer . . . my son . . . bring me . . . a drop of coffee. . . ."

I ran to him.

"Father! I've been looking for you for so long. . . . Where were you? Did you sleep? . . . How do you feel?"

He was burning with fever. Like a wild beast, I cleared a way for myself to the coffee cauldron. And I managed to carry back a cupful. I had a sip. The rest was for him. I can't forget the light of thankfulness in his eyes while he gulped it down—an animal gratitude. With those few gulps of hot water, I probably brought him more satisfaction than I had done during my whole childhood.

He was lying on a plank, livid, his lips pale and dried up, shaken by tremors. I could not stay by him for long. Orders had been given to clear the place for cleaning. Only the sick could stay.

We stayed outside for five hours. Soup was given out. As soon as we were allowed to go back to the blocks, I ran to my father.

"Have you had anything to eat?"

"No."

"Why not?"

"They didn't give us anything . . . they said that if we were ill we should die soon anyway and it would be a pity to waste the food. I can't go on any more. . . ."

I gave him what was left of my soup. But it was with a heavy heart. I felt that I was giving it up to him against my will. No better than Rabbi Eliahou's son had I withstood the test.

He grew weaker day by day, his gaze veiled, his face the color of dead leaves. On the third day after our arrival at Buchenwald, everyone had to go to the showers. Even the sick, who had to go through last.

On the way back from the baths, we had to wait outside for a long time. They had not yet finished cleaning the blocks.

Seeing my father in the distance, I ran to meet him. He went by me like a ghost, passed me without stopping, without looking at me. I called to him. He did not come back. I ran after him:

"Father, where are you running to?"

He looked at me for a moment, and his gaze was distant, visionary; it was the face of someone else. A moment only and on he ran again.

Struck down with dysentery, my father lay in his bunk, five other invalids with him. I sat by his side, watching him, not daring to believe that he could escape death again. Nevertheless, I did all I could to give him hope.

Suddenly, he raised himself on his bunk and put his feverish lips to my ear:

"Eliezer . . . I must tell you where to find the gold and the money I buried . . . in the cellar. . . . You know. . . ."

He began to talk faster and faster, as though he were afraid he would not have time to tell me. I tried to explain to him that this was not the end, that we would go back to the house together, but he would not listen to me. He could no longer listen to me. He was exhausted. A trickle of saliva, mingled with blood, was running from between his lips. He had closed his eyes. His breath was coming in gasps.

For a ration of bread, I managed to change beds with a prisoner in my father's bunk. In the afternoon the doctor came. I went and told him that my father was very ill.

"Bring him here!"

I explained that he could not stand up. But the doctor refused to listen to anything. Somehow, I brought my father to him. He stared at him, then questioned him in a clipped voice:

"What do you want?"

"My father's ill," I answered for him. "Dysentery . . ."

"Dysentery? That's not my business. I'm a surgeon. Go on! Make room for the others."

Protests did no good.

"I can't go on, son. . . . Take me back to my bunk. . . ."

I took him back and helped him to lie down. He was shivering.

"Try and sleep a bit, father. Try to go to sleep. . . ."

His breathing was labored, thick. He kept his eyes shut. Yet I was convinced that he could see everything, that now he could see the truth in all things.

Another doctor came to the block. But my father would not get up. He knew that it was useless.

Besides, this doctor had only come to finish off the sick. I could hear him shouting at them that they were lazy and just wanted to stay in bed. I felt like leaping at his throat, strangling him. But I no longer had the courage or the strength. I was riveted to my father's deathbed. My hands hurt, I was clenching them so hard. Oh, to strangle the doctor and the others! To burn the whole world! My father's murderers! But the cry stayed in my throat.

When I came back from the bread distribution, I found my father weeping like a child:

"Son, they keep hitting me!"

"Who?"

I thought he was delirious.

"Him, the Frenchman . . . and the Pole . . . they were hitting me."

Another wound to the heart, another hate, another reason for living lost.

"Eliezer . . . Eliezer . . . tell them not to hit me. . . . I haven't done anything. . . . Why do they keep hitting me?"

I began to abuse his neighbors. They laughed at me. I promised them bread, soup. They laughed. Then they got angry;

they could not stand my father any longer, they said, because he was now unable to drag himself outside to relieve himself.

The following day he complained that they had taken his ration of bread.

"While you were asleep?"

"No. I wasn't asleep. They jumped on top of me. They snatched my bread . . . and they hit me . . . again. . . . I can't stand any more, son . . . a drop of water. . . ."

I knew that he must not drink. But he pleaded with me for so long that I gave in. Water was the worst poison he could have, but what else could I do for him? With water, without water, it would all be over soon anyway. . . .

"You, at least, have some mercy on me. . . ."

Have mercy on him! I, his only son!

A week went by like this.

"This is your father, isn't it?" asked the head of the block.

"Yes."

"He's very ill."

"The doctor won't do anything for him."

"The doctor *can't* do anything for him, now. And neither can you."

He put his great hairy hand on my shoulder and added:

"Listen to me, boy. Don't forget that you're in a concentration camp. Here, every man has to fight for himself and not think of anyone else. Even of his father. Here, there are no fathers, no brothers, no friends. Everyone lives and dies for himself alone. I'll give you a sound piece of advice—don't give your ration of bread and soup to your old father. There's nothing you can do for him. And you're killing yourself. Instead, you ought to be having his ration."

I listened to him without interrupting. He was right, I thought in the most secret region of my heart, but I dared not admit it. It's too late to save your old father, I said to myself. You ought to be having two rations of bread, two rations of soup. . . .

Only a fraction of a second, but I felt guilty. I ran to find a little soup to give my father. But he did not want it. All he wanted was water.

"Don't drink water . . . have some soup. . . ."

"I'm burning . . . why are you being so unkind to me, my son? Some water. . . ."

I brought him some water. Then I left the block for roll call. But I turned around and came back again. I lay down on the top bunk. Invalids were allowed to stay in the block. So I would be an invalid myself. I would not leave my father.

There was silence all round now, broken only by groans. In front of the block, the SS were giving orders. An officer passed by the beds. My father begged me:

"My son, some water. . . . I'm burning. . . . My stomach. . . ."

"Quiet, over there!" yelled the officer.

"Eliezer," went on my father, "some water. . . ."

The officer came up to him and shouted at him to be quiet. But my father did not hear him. He went on calling me. The officer dealt him a violent blow on the head with his truncheon.

I did not move. I was afraid. My body was afraid of also receiving a blow.

Then my father made a rattling noise and it was my name: "Eliezer."

I could see that he was still breathing—spasmodically.

I did not move.

When I got down after roll call, I could see his lips trembling as he murmured something. Bending over him, I stayed gazing at him for over an hour, engraving into myself the picture of his blood-stained face, his shattered skull.

Then I had to go to bed. I climbed into my bunk, above my father, who was still alive. It was January 28, 1945.

I awoke on January 29 at dawn. In my father's place lay another invalid. They must have taken him away before dawn and carried him to the crematory. He may still have been breathing.

There were no prayers at his grave. No candles were lit to his memory. His last word was my name. A summons, to which I did not respond.

I did not weep, and it pained me that I could not weep. But I had no more tears. And, in the depths of my being, in the recesses of my weakened conscience, could I have searched it, I might perhaps have found something like—free at last!

9

I HAD to stay at Buchenwald until April eleventh. I have nothing to say of my life during this period. It no longer mattered. After my father's death, nothing could touch me any more.

I was transferred to the children's block, where there were six hundred of us.

The front was drawing nearer.

I spent my days in a state of total idleness. And I had but one desire—to eat. I no longer thought of my father or of my mother.

From time to time I would dream of a drop of soup, of an extra ration of soup. . . .

On April fifth, the wheel of history turned.

It was late in the afternoon. We were standing in the block, waiting for an SS man to come and count us. He was late in coming. Such a delay was unknown till then in the history of Buchenwald. Something must have happened.

Two hours later the loudspeakers sent out an order from the head of the camp: all the Jews must come to the assembly place.

This was the end! Hitler was going to keep his promise.

The children in our block went toward the place. There was nothing else we could do. Gustav, the head of the block, made this clear to us with his truncheon. But on the way we met some prisoners who whispered to us:

"Go back to your block. The Germans are going to shoot you. Go back to your block, and don't move."

We went back to our block. We learned on the way that the camp resistance organization had decided not to abandon the Jews and was going to prevent their being liquidated.

As it was late and there was great upheaval—innumerable Jews had passed themselves off as non-Jews—the head of the camp decided that a general roll call would take place the following day. Everybody would have to be present.

The roll call took place. The head of the camp announced that Buchenwald was to be liquidated. Ten blocks of deportees would be evacuated each day. From this moment, there would be no further distribution of bread and soup. And the evacuation began. Every day, several thousand prisoners went through the camp gate and never came back.

On April tenth, there were still about twenty thousand of us in the camp, including several hundred children. They decided to evacuate us all at once, right on until the evening. Afterward, they were going to blow up the camp.

So we were massed in the huge assembly square, in rows of five, waiting to see the gate open. Suddenly, the sirens began to wail. An alert! We went back to the blocks. It was too late to evacuate us that evening. The evacuation was postponed again to the following day.

We were tormented with hunger. We had eaten nothing for six days, except a bit of grass or some potato peelings found near the kitchens.

At ten o'clock in the morning the SS scattered through the camp, moving the last victims toward the assembly place.

Then the resistance movement decided to act. Armed men suddenly rose up everywhere. Bursts of firing. Grenades exploding. We children stayed flat on the ground in the block.

The battle did not last long. Toward noon everything was quiet again. The SS had fled and the resistance had taken charge of the running of the camp.

At about six o'clock in the evening, the first American tank stood at the gates of Buchenwald.

Our first act as free men was to throw ourselves onto the provisions. We thought only of that. Not of revenge, not of our families. Nothing but bread.

And even when we were no longer hungry, there was still no one who thought of revenge. On the following day, some of the young men went to Weimar to get some potatoes and clothes, and to sleep with girls. But of revenge, not a sign.

Three days after the liberation of Buchenwald I became very ill with food poisoning. I was transferred to the hospital and spent two weeks between life and death.

One day I was able to get up, after gathering all my strength. I wanted to see myself in the mirror hanging on the opposite wall. I had not seen myself since the ghetto.

From the depths of the mirror, a corpse gazed back at me.

The look in his eyes, as they stared into mine, has never left me.

Connected
Readings

All the Unburied Ones

Anna Akhmatova

Translated by Judith Hemschemeyer

All the unburied ones—I buried them,
I mourned for them all, but who will mourn for me?

A Jewish Cemetery Near Leningrad

Josef Brodsky

Translated by Keith Bosley

A Jewish cemetery near Leningrad.
A crooked fence of rotten plywood.
Behind the crooked fence lie side by side
lawyers, merchants, musicians, revolutionaries.
For themselves they sang.
For themselves they saved.
For others they died.
But first they paid the taxes
                              respected the law
and in this unavoidably material world
pored over the Talmud
                         idealists to the end.

Perhaps they saw further.
Perhaps they believed blindly.
But they taught their sons to be patient
                                   and to endure.
They sowed no grain.
                      They never sowed grain.
They just laid themselves in the cold earth
                                   like seeds.
And fell asleep forever.
Then they were covered over with earth
candles were lit
and on the Day of Remembrance
hungry old men with shrill voices
choking with cold
shouted about peace.

And they got it.
                    In the form of material decay.
Remembering nothing.
Forgetting nothing.
Behind a crooked fence of wet plywood.
A couple of miles from the tram terminus.

Bitburg

Elie Wiesel

*Elie Wiesel rebuilt his life with startling suc-
cess after the Holocaust. He has gained world-
wide recognition, both as an author and as a
leader in the Jewish community. A winner of the
Nobel Peace Prize, Wiesel is often sought after
by world leaders for his opinions.*

Introduction by William Safire

Elie Wiesel, who lost his family to Nazi genocide, came to
the United States from his native Romania in 1956 to "bear
witness" to the Holocaust, or Shoah. In novels and nonfiction
writings in France and the United States, and in talks before
audiences around the world, the quiet-voiced Wiesel reminds
listeners and readers of unspeakable crimes and inexplicable
silence.

In 1985, President Ronald Reagan planned a state visit
to West Germany, its purpose to acknowledge the importance of that country's membership in the alliance of free
nations and to help Germans bury their own guilty past.
Among the ceremonies planned by Chancellor Helmut Kohl
and the White House staff was a visit to a cemetery in Bitburg, near a U.S. military installation. After the schedule
was announced, it was discovered that among the graves
were several of members of Hitler's Waffen SS, notorious for
their anti-Semitism. Mr. Kohl let it be known that he and
most Germans would be offended at a cancellation; many
Jews in the United States took offense at the insensitive
scheduling.

Mr. Reagan decided to go ahead with the visit to Bitburg—
there to pointedly turn his back at the Nazi graves—but first
he gave Elie Wiesel, then chairman of the U.S. Holocaust
Memorial Council, the opportunity to present his objection
publicly to the president at a White House ceremony present-
ing him with a medal of achievement. Gently, and with ap-
propriate respect, the Jewish leader showed why the decision to visit Bitburg had been a mistake.

MR. PRESIDENT, . . . I am grateful to you for the medal. But this medal is not mine alone. It belongs to all those who remember what SS killers have done to their victims.

It was given to me by the American people for my writings, teaching and for my testimony. When I write, I feel my invisible teachers standing over my shoulders, reading my words and judging their veracity. And while I feel responsible for the living, I feel equally responsible to the dead. Their memory dwells in my memory.

Forty years ago, a young man awoke, and he found himself an orphan in an orphaned world. What have I learned in the last forty years? Small things. I learned the perils of language and those of silence. I learned that in extreme situations when human lives and dignity are at stake, neutrality is a sin. It helps the killers, not the victims. I learned the meaning of solitude, Mr. President. We were alone, desperately alone.

Today is April 19, and [on] April 19, 1943, the Warsaw Ghetto rose in arms against the onslaught of the Nazis. They were so few and so young and so helpless. And nobody came to their help. And they had to fight what was then the mightiest legion in Europe. Every underground received help except the Jewish underground. And yet they managed to fight and resist and push back those Nazis and their accomplices for six weeks. And yet the leaders of the free world, Mr. President, knew everything and did so little, or nothing, or at least nothing specifically to save Jewish children from death. You spoke of Jewish children, Mr. President. One million Jewish children perished. If I spent my entire life reciting their names, I would die before finishing the task.

Mr. President, I have seen children, I have seen them being thrown in the flames alive. Words, they die on my lips. So I have learned, I have learned, I have learned the fragility of the human condition.

And I am reminded of a great moral essayist. The gentle and forceful Abe Rosenthal, having visited Auschwitz, once wrote an extraordinary reportage about the persecution of Jews, and he called it "Forgive them not, Father, for they knew what they did."

I have learned that the Holocaust was a unique and uniquely Jewish event, albeit with universal implications. Not all victims were Jews. But all Jews were victims. I have learned the danger of indifference, the crime of indifference. For the opposite of love, I have learned, is not hate, but indifference. Jews were killed by the enemy but betrayed by their so-called allies, who found political reasons to justify their indifference or passivity.

But I have also learned that suffering confers no privileges. It all depends what one does with it. And this is why survivors, of whom you spoke, Mr. President, have tried to teach their contemporaries how to build on ruins, how to invent hope in a world that offers none, how to proclaim faith to a generation that has seen it shamed and mutilated. And I believe, we believe, that memory is the answer, perhaps the only answer.

A few days ago, on the anniversary of the liberation of Buchenwald, all of us, Americans, watched with dismay and anger as the Soviet Union and East Germany distorted both past and present history.

Mr. President, I was there. I was there when American liberators arrived. And they gave us back our lives. And what I felt for them then nourishes me to the end of my days and will do so. If you only knew what we tried to do with them then. We who were so weak that we couldn't carry our own lives, we tried to carry them in triumph.

Mr. President, we are grateful to the American army for liberating us. We are grateful to this country, the greatest democracy in the world, the freest nation in the world, the moral nation, the authority in the world. And we are grateful, especially, to this country for having offered us haven and refuge, and grateful to its leadership for being so friendly to Israel.

And, Mr. President, do you know that the ambassador of Israel, who sits next to you, who is my friend, and has been for so many years, is himself a survivor? And if you knew all the causes we fought together for the last thirty years, you should be prouder of him. And we are proud of him.

And we are grateful, of course, to Israel. We are eternally grateful to Israel for existing. We needed Israel in 1948 as we need it now. And we are grateful to Congress for its continuous philosophy of humanism and compassion for the underprivileged.

And as for yourself, Mr. President, we are so grateful to you for being a friend of the Jewish people, for trying to help the oppressed Jews in the Soviet Union. And to do whatever we can to save Shcharansky and Abe Stolar and Iosif Begun and Sakharov and all the dissidents who need freedom. And of course, we thank you for your support of the Jewish state of Israel.

But, Mr. President, I wouldn't be the person I am, and you wouldn't respect me for what I am, if I were not to tell you also of the sadness that is in my heart for what happened during the last week. And I am sure that you, too, are sad for the same reasons.

What can I do? I belong to a traumatized generation. And to us, as to you, symbols are important. And furthermore, following our ancient tradition, and we are speaking about Jewish heritage, our tradition commands us "to speak truth to power."

So may I speak to you, Mr. President, with respect and admiration, of the events that happened?

We have met four or five times. And each time I came away enriched, for I know of your commitment to humanity.

And therefore I am convinced, as you have told us earlier when we spoke, that you were not aware of the presence of SS graves in the Bitburg cemetery. Of course you didn't know. But now we all are aware.

May I, Mr. President, if it's possible at all, implore you to do something else, to find a way, to find another way, another site? That place, Mr. President, is not your place. Your place is with the victims of the SS.

Oh, we know there are political and strategic reasons, but this issue, as all issues related to that awesome event, transcends politics and diplomacy.

The issue here is not politics, but good and evil. And we must never confuse them.

For I have seen the SS at work. And I have seen their victims. They were my friends. They were my parents.

Mr. President, there was a degree of suffering and loneliness in the concentration camps that defies imagination. Cut off from the world with no refuge anywhere, sons watched helplessly their fathers being beaten to death. Mothers watched their children die of hunger. And then there was Mengele and his selections. Terror, fear, isolation, torture, gas chambers, flames, flames rising to the heavens.

But, Mr. President, I know and I understand, we all do, that you seek reconciliation. And so do I, so do we. And I too wish to attain true reconciliation with the German people. I do not believe in collective guilt, nor in collective responsibility. Only the killers were guilty. Their sons and daughters are not.

And I believe, Mr. President, that we can and we must work together with them and with all people. And we must work to bring peace and understanding to a tormented world that, as you know, is still awaiting redemption.

I thank you, Mr. President.

from
Survival in Auschwitz

Primo Levi

Author Primo Levi was arrested in Italy as a member of the anti-Fascist resistance. He was sentenced to Auschwitz in 1944. Seeing the horrors that surrounded him, Levi despaired.

I MUST confess it: after only one week of prison, the instinct for cleanliness disappeared in me. I wander aimlessly around the washroom when I suddenly see Steinlauf, my friend aged almost fifty, with nude torso, scrub his neck and shoulders with little success (he has no soap) but great energy. Steinlauf sees me and greets me, and without preamble asks me severely why I do not wash. Why should I wash? Would I be better off than I am? Would I please someone more? Would I live a day, an hour longer? I would probably live a shorter time, because to wash is an effort, a waste of energy and warmth. Does not Steinlauf know that after half an hour with the coal sacks every difference between him and me will have disappeared? The more I think about it, the more washing one's face in our condition seems a stupid feat, even frivolous: a mechanical habit, or worse, a dismal repetition of an extinct rite. We will all die, we are all about to die: if they give me ten minutes between the reveille and work, I want to dedicate them to something else, to draw into myself, to weigh up things, or merely to look at the sky and think that I am looking at it perhaps for the last time; or even to let myself live, to indulge myself in the luxury of an idle moment.

But Steinlauf interrupts me. He has finished washing and is now drying himself with his cloth jacket which he was holding before wrapped up between his knees and which he will soon put on. And without interrupting the operation he administers me a complete lesson.

It grieves me now that I have forgotten his plain, outspoken words, the words of ex-sergeant Steinlauf of the Austro-Hungarian army, Iron Cross of the '14–'18 war. It grieves me because it means that I have to translate his uncertain Italian and his quiet manner of speaking of a good soldier into my language of an incredulous man. But this was the sense, not forgotten either then or later: that precisely because the Lager [prison camp] was a great machine to reduce us to beasts, we must not become beasts; that even in this place one can survive, and therefore one must want to survive, to tell the story, to bear witness; and that to survive we must force ourselves to save at least the skeleton, the scaffolding, the form of civilization. We are slaves, deprived of every right, exposed to every insult, condemned to certain death, but we still possess one power, and we must defend it with all our strength for it is the last—the power to refuse our consent. So we must certainly wash our faces without soap in dirty water and dry ourselves on our jackets. We must polish our shoes, not because the regulation states it, but for dignity and propriety. We must walk erect, without dragging our feet, not in homage to Prussian [German] discipline but to remain alive, not to begin to die.

These things Steinlauf, a man of good will, told me; strange things to my unaccustomed ear, understood and accepted only in part. . . .

from
The Diary of a Young Girl

Anne Frank

*On Friday, June 12, 1942, thirteen-year-old Anne Frank
received a diary for her birthday. Shortly after, she and her
family went into hiding to escape persecution by the Nazis.
Their chosen place, where they would live for the next couple
of years, was a hidden room attached to the warehouse
where her father once worked. They were soon joined by Mr.
and Mrs. Van Daan, their son Peter, and Mr. Dussel.*

*Calling the diary "Kitty," Anne recorded her thoughts and
feelings on the events around her. Her diary remains one of
the greatest testaments to the suffering caused by the Nazis.*

Saturday, 27 November, 1943

Dear Kitty,

Yesterday evening, before I fell asleep, who should suddenly
appear before my eyes but Lies!

I saw her in front of me, clothed in rags, her face thin and
worn. Her eyes were very big and she looked so sadly and reproachfully at me that I could read in her eyes: "Oh Anne, why
have you deserted me? Help, oh, help me, rescue me from this
hell!"

And I cannot help her, I can only look on, how others suffer
and die, and can only pray to God to send her back to us.

I just saw Lies, no one else, and now I understand. I mis-
judged her and was too young to understand her difficulties.
She was attached to a new girl friend, and to her it seemed as
though I wanted to take her away. What the poor girl must have
felt like, I know; I know the feeling so well myself!

Sometimes, in a flash, I saw something of her life, but a moment later I was selfishly absorbed again in my own pleasures
and problems. It was horrid of me to treat her as I did, and now
she looked at me, oh so helplessly, with her pale face and im-
ploring eyes. If only I could help her!

Oh, God, that I should have all I could wish for and that she
should be seized by such a terrible fate. I am not more virtuous

than she; she, too, wanted to do what was right, why should I be chosen to live and she probably to die? What was the difference between us? Why are we so far from each other now?

Quite honestly, I haven't thought about her for months, yes, almost for a year. Not completely forgotten her, but still I had never thought about her like this, until I saw her before me in all her misery.

Oh, Lies, I hope that, if you live until the end of the war, you will come back to us and that I shall be able to take you in and do something to make up for the wrong I did you.

But when I am able to help her again, then she will not need my help so badly as now. I wonder if she ever thinks of me; if so, what would she feel?

Good Lord, defend her, so that at least she is not alone. Oh, if only You could tell her that I think lovingly of her and with sympathy, perhaps that would give her greater endurance.

I must not go on thinking about it, because I don't get any further. I only keep seeing her great big eyes, and cannot free myself from them. I wonder if Lies has real faith in herself, and not only what has been thrust upon her?

I don't even know, I never took the trouble to ask her!

Lies, Lies, if only I could take you away, if only I could let you share all the things I enjoy. It is too late now, I can't help, or repair the wrong I have done. But I shall never forget her again, and I shall always pray for her.

Yours, Anne

Tuesday, 11 April, 1944

Dear Kitty,

. . . At half past nine Peter knocked softly on the door and asked Daddy if he would just help him upstairs over a difficult English sentence. "That's a blind," I said to Margot, "anyone could see through that one!" I was right. They were in the act of breaking into the warehouse. Daddy, Van Daan, Dussel, and Peter were downstairs in a flash. Margot, Mummy, Mrs. Van Daan, and I stayed upstairs and waited.

Four frightened women just have to talk, so talk we did, until we heard a bang downstairs. After that all was quiet, the clock struck a quarter to ten. The color had vanished from our faces, we were still quiet, although we were afraid. Where could the men be? What was that bang? Would they be fighting the burglars?

Ten o'clock, footsteps on the stairs: Daddy, white and nervous, entered, followed by Mr. Van Daan. "Lights out, creep upstairs, we expect the police in the house!"

There was no time to be frightened: the lights went out, I quickly grabbed a jacket, and we were upstairs. "What has happened? Tell us quickly!" There was no one to tell us, the men having disappeared downstairs again. Only at ten past ten did they reappear; two kept watch at Peter's open window, the door to the landing was closed, the swinging cupboard shut. We hung a jersey round the night light, and after that they told us:

Peter heard two loud bangs on the landing, ran downstairs, and saw there was a large plank out of the left half of the door. He dashed upstairs, warned the "Home Guard" of the family, and the four of them proceeded downstairs. When they entered the warehouse, the burglars were in the act of enlarging the hole. Without further thought Van Daan shouted: "Police!"

A few hurried steps outside, and the burglars had fled. In order to avoid the hole being noticed by the police, a plank was put against it, but a good hard kick from outside sent it flying to the ground. The men were perplexed at such impudence, and both Van Daan and Peter felt murder welling up within them; Van Daan beat on the ground with a chopper, and all was quiet again. Once more they wanted to put the plank in front of the hole. Disturbance! A married couple outside shone a torch through the opening, lighting up the whole warehouse. "Hell!" muttered one of the men, and now they switched over from their role of police to that of burglars. The four of them sneaked upstairs, Peter quickly opened the doors and windows of the kitchen and private office, flung the telephone onto the floor, and finally the four of them landed behind the swinging cupboard.

END OF PART ONE

The married couple with the torch would probably have warned the police: it was Sunday evening, Easter Sunday, no one at the office on Easter Monday, so none of us could budge until Tuesday morning. Think of it, waiting in such fear for two nights and a day! No one had anything to suggest, so we simply sat there in pitch-darkness, because Mrs. Van Daan in her fright had unintentionally turned the lamp right out; talked in whispers, and at every creak one heard "Sh! sh!"

It turned half past ten, eleven, but not a sound; Daddy and

Van Daan joined us in turns. Then a quarter past eleven, a bustle and noise downstairs. Everyone's breath was audible, otherwise no one moved. Footsteps in the house, in the private office, kitchen, then . . . on our staircase. No one breathed audibly now, footsteps on our staircase, then a rattling of the swinging cupboard. This moment is indescribable. "Now we are lost!" I said, and could see us all being taken away by the Gestapo that very night. Twice they rattled at the cupboard, then there was nothing, the footsteps withdrew, we were saved so far. A shiver seemed to pass from one to another, I heard someone's teeth chattering, no one said a word.

There was not another sound in the house, but a light was burning on our landing, right in front of the cupboard. Could that be because it was a secret cupboard? Perhaps the police had forgotten the light? Would someone come back to put it out? Tongues loosened, there was no one in the house any longer, perhaps there was someone on guard outside.

Next we did three things: we went over again what we supposed had happened, we trembled with fear, and we had to go to the lavatory. The buckets were in the attic, so all we had was Peter's tin wastepaper basket. Van Daan went first, then Daddy, but Mummy was too shy to face it. Daddy brought the wastepaper basket into the room, where Margot, Mrs. Van Daan, and I gladly made use of it. Finally Mummy decided to do so too. People kept on asking for paper—fortunately I had some in my pocket!

The tin smelled ghastly, everything went on in a whisper, we were tired, it was twelve o'clock. "Lie down on the floor then and sleep." Margot and I were each given a pillow and one blanket; Margot lying just near the store cupboard and I between the table legs. The smell wasn't quite so bad when one was on the floor, but still Mrs. Van Daan quietly brought some chlorine, a tea towel over the pot serving as a second expedient.

Talk, whispers, fear, stink, flatulation, and always someone on the pot; then try to go to sleep! However, by half past two I was so tired that I knew no more until half past three. I awoke when Mrs. Van Daan laid her head on my foot.

"For heaven's sake, give me something to put on!" I asked. I was given something, but don't ask what—a pair of woolen knickers over my pajamas, a red jumper, and a black skirt, white oversocks and a pair of sports stockings full of holes. Then Mrs. Van Daan sat in the chair and her husband came and lay on my feet. I lay thinking till half past three, shivering the whole time, which prevented Van Daan from sleeping. I prepared myself for the return of the police, then we'd have to say that we were in hiding; they would either be good Dutch people, then we'd be saved, or N.S.B.-ers, then we'd have to bribe them!

"In that case, destroy the radio," sighed Mrs. Van Daan. "Yes, in the stove!" replied her husband. "If they find us, then let them find the radio as well!"

"Then they will find Anne's diary," added Daddy. "Burn it then," suggested the most terrified member of the party. This, and when the police rattled the cupboard door, were my worst moments. "Not my diary; if my diary goes, I go with it!" But luckily Daddy didn't answer.

There is no object in recounting all the conversations that I can still remember; so much was said. I comforted Mrs. Van Daan, who was very scared. We talked about escaping and being questioned by the Gestapo, about ringing up, and being brave.

"We must behave like soldiers, Mrs. Van Daan. If all is up now, then let's go for Queen and Country, for freedom, truth, and right, as they always say on the Dutch News from England. The only thing that is really rotten is that we get a lot of other people into trouble too."

Mr. Van Daan changed places again with his wife after an hour, and Daddy came and sat beside me. The men smoked non-stop, now and then there was a deep sigh, then someone went on the pot and everything began all over again.

Four o'clock, five o'clock, half past five. Then I went and sat with Peter by his window and listened, so close together that we could feel each other's bodies quivering; we spoke a word or two now and then, and listened attentively. In the room next door they took down the blackout. They wanted to call up Koophuis at seven o'clock and get him to send someone around. Then they wrote down everything they wanted to tell Koophuis over the phone. The risk that the police on guard at the door, or in the warehouse, might hear the telephone was very great, but the danger of the police returning was even greater.

The points were these:

Burglars broken in: police have been in the house, as far as the swinging cupboard, but no further.

Burglars apparently disturbed, forced open the door in the warehouse and escaped through the garden.

Main entrance bolted, Kraler must have used the second door when he left. The typewriters and adding machine are safe in the black case in the private office.

Try to warn Henk and fetch the key from Elli, then go and look round the office—on the pretext of feeding the cat.

Everything went according to plan. Koophuis was phoned, the typewriters which we had upstairs were put in the case. Then we sat around the table again and waited for Henk or the police.

Peter had fallen asleep and Van Daan and I were lying on the floor, when we heard loud footsteps downstairs. I got up quietly: "That's Henk."

"No, no, it's the police," some of the others said.

Someone knocked at the door, Miep whistled. This was too much for Mrs. Van Daan, she turned as white as a sheet and sank limply into a chair; had the tension lasted one minute longer she would have fainted.

Our room was a perfect picture when Miep and Henk entered, the table alone would have been worth photographing! A copy of *Cinema and Theater,* covered with jam and a remedy for diarrhea, opened at a page of dancing girls, two jam pots, two started loaves of bread, a mirror, comb, matches, ash, cigarettes, tobacco, ash tray, books, a pair of pants, a torch, toilet paper, etc., etc., lay jumbled together in variegated splendor.

Of course Henk and Miep were greeted with shouts and tears. Henk mended the hole in the door with some planks, and soon went off again to inform the police of the burglary. Miep had also found a letter under the warehouse door from the night watchman Slagter, who had noticed the hole and warned the police, whom he would also visit.

So we had half an hour to tidy ourselves. I've never seen such a change take place in half an hour. Margot and I took the bedclothes downstairs, went to the W.C., washed, and did our teeth and hair. After that I tidied the room a bit and went upstairs again. The table there was already cleared, so we ran off some water and made coffee and tea, boiled the milk, and laid the table for lunch. Daddy and Peter emptied the potties and cleaned them with warm water and chlorine. . . .

Now there are debates going on all the time in the "Secret Annex." Kraler reproached us for our carelessness. Henk, too, said that in a case like that we must never go downstairs. We have been pointedly reminded that we are in hiding, that we are Jews in chains, chained to one spot, without any rights, but with a thousand duties. We Jews mustn't show our feelings, must be brave and strong, must accept all inconveniences and not grumble, must do what is within our power and trust in God. Sometime this terrible war will be over. Surely the time will come when we are people again, and not just Jews.

Who has inflicted this upon us? Who has made us Jews different from all other people? Who has allowed us to suffer so terribly up till now? It is God that has made us as we are, but it will be God, too, who will raise us up again. If we bear all this suffering and if there are still Jews left, when it is over, then Jews, instead of being doomed, will be held up as an example. Who knows, it might even be our religion from which the world and all peoples learn good, and for that reason and that reason only do we have to suffer now. We can never become just Netherlanders, or just English, or representatives of any country for that matter, we will always remain Jews, but we want to, too.

Be brave! Let us remain aware of our task and not grumble, a solution will come, God has never deserted our people. Right through the ages there have been Jews, through all the ages they have had to suffer, but it has made them strong too; the weak fall, but the strong will remain and never go under!

During that night I really felt that I had to die, I waited for the police, I was prepared, as the soldier is on the battlefield. I was eager to lay down my life for the country, but now, now I've been saved again, now my first wish after the war is that I may become Dutch! I love the Dutch, I love this country, I love the language and want to work here. And even if I have to write to the Queen myself, I will not give up until I have reached my goal.

I am becoming still more independent of my parents, young as I am, I face life with more courage than Mummy; my feeling for justice is immovable, and truer than hers. I know what I want, I have a goal, an opinion, I have a religion and love. Let me be myself and then I am satisfied. I know that I'm a woman, a woman with inward strength and plenty of courage.

If God lets me live, I shall attain more than Mummy ever has done, I shall not remain insignificant, I shall work in the world and for mankind!

And now I know that first and foremost I shall require courage and cheerfulness!

Yours, Anne

Tuesday, 1 August, 1944

Dear Kitty,

"Little bundle of contradictions." That's how I ended my last letter and that's how I'm going to begin this one. "A little bundle of contradictions," can you tell me exactly what it is? What does contradiction mean? Like so many words, it can mean two things, contradiction from without and contradiction from within.

The first is the ordinary "not giving in easily, always knowing best, getting in the last word," *enfin,* all the unpleasant qualities for which I'm renowned. The second nobody knows about, that's my own secret.

I've already told you before that I have, as it were, a dual personality. One half embodies my exuberant cheerfulness, making fun of everything, my high-spiritedness, and above all, the way I take everything lightly. This includes not taking offense at a flirtation, a kiss, an embrace, a dirty joke. This side is usually lying in wait and pushes away the other, which is much better, deeper and purer. You must realize that no one knows Anne's better side and that's why most people find me so insufferable.

Certainly I'm a giddy clown for one afternoon, but then everyone's had enough of me for another month. Really, it's just the same as a love film is for deep-thinking people, simply a diversion, amusing just for once, something which is soon forgotten, not bad, but certainly not good. I loathe having to tell you this, but why shouldn't I, if I know it's true anyway? My lighter superficial side will always be too quick for the deeper side of me and that's why it will always win. You can't imagine how often I've already tried to push this Anne away, to cripple her, to hide her, because after all, she's only half of what's called Anne: but it doesn't work and I know, too, why it doesn't work.

I'm awfully scared that everyone who knows me as I always am will discover that I have another side, a finer and better side. I'm afraid they'll laugh at me, think I'm ridiculous and sentimental, not take me seriously. I'm used to not being taken seriously but it's only the "lighthearted" Anne that's used to it and can bear it; the "deeper" Anne is too frail for it. Sometimes, if I really compel the good Anne to take the stage for a quarter of an hour, she simply shrivels up as soon as she has to speak, and lets Anne number one take over, and before I realize it, she has disappeared.

Therefore, the nice Anne is never present in company, has not appeared one single time so far, but almost always predominates when we're alone. I know exactly how I'd like to be, how I am too . . . inside. But, alas, I'm only like that for myself. And perhaps that's why, no, I'm sure it's the reason why I say I've got a happy nature within and why other people think I've got a happy nature without. I am guided by the pure Anne within, but outside I'm nothing but a frolicsome little goat who's broken loose.

As I've already said, I never utter my real feelings about anything and that's how I've acquired the name of chaser-after-boys, flirt, know-all, reader of love stories. The cheerful Anne laughs about it, gives cheeky answers, shrugs her shoulders indifferently, behaves as if she doesn't care, but, oh dearie me, the quiet Anne's reactions are just the opposite. If I'm to be quite honest, then I must admit that it does hurt me, that I try terribly hard to change myself, but that I'm always fighting against a more powerful enemy.

A voice sobs within me: "There you are, that's what's become of you: you're uncharitable, you look supercilious and peevish, people dislike you and all because you won't listen to the advice given you by your own better half." Oh, I would like to listen, but it doesn't work; if I'm quiet and serious, everyone thinks it's a new comedy and then I have to get out of it by turning it into a joke, not to mention my own family, who are sure to think I'm ill, make me swallow pills for headaches and nerves, feel my neck and my head to see whether I'm running a temperature, ask if I'm constipated and criticize me for being in a bad mood. I can't keep that up: if I'm watched to that extent, I start by getting snappy, then unhappy, and finally I twist my heart round again, so that the bad is on the outside and the good is on the inside and keep on trying to find a way of becoming what I would so like to be, and what I could be, if . . . there weren't any other people living in the world.

Yours, Anne

(Afterword by Ernst Schnabel)

ON August 4, 1944, following information provided by a Dutch informer, the Gestapo penetrated into the Franks' hiding place. The eight Jews, together with Mr. Koophuis and Mr. Kraler, were taken to Gestapo headquarters in Amsterdam. After a few weeks' imprisonment, Mr. Koophuis was released for medical care. Mr. Kraler spent eight months in a forced labor camp. The Franks, the Van Daans, and Mr. Dussel were sent to Westerbork.

On September 3, the day the Allies captured Brussels, these

eight were among the last shipment of a thousand Jews to leave Holland. The prisoners were herded aboard a freight train, seventy-five people to a car. The cars, each with only a small, barred window high on one side, were sealed. For three days and nights the train wandered eastward across Germany, often stopping, backing, detouring. On the third night it reached Auschwitz in Poland. In the glare of searchlights, watched by black-uniformed SS men tightly reining their police dogs, the Jews left the train. On the platform men and women were separated. It was the last Otto Frank saw of his family.

At Auschwitz the healthier prisoners, their heads shaved, worked twelve hours a day digging sod, driven relentlessly by the sadistic *Kapos*, criminals who served the SS as labor overseers. At night they were locked into crowded barracks. Outside the windows they could see the sky glow red above the crematories.

Through the research of Ernst Schnabel, a German writer whose book *Anne Frank, A Portrait in Courage* was published in 1958, some of the events of the last few months of Anne's life have been reconstructed. Auschwitz, a former inmate told Mr. Schnabel, was "'a fantastically well-organized, spick-and-span hell. The food was bad, but it was distributed regularly. We kept our barracks so clean that you could have eaten off the floor. Anyone who died in the barracks was taken away first thing in the morning. Anyone who fell ill disappeared also. Those who were gassed did not scream. They just were no longer there. The crematories smoked, but we received our rations and had roll calls. The SS harassed us at roll call and kept guard with machine guns from the watchtowers, and the camp fences were charged with high-tension electricity, but we could wash every day and sometimes even take showers. If you could forget the gas chambers, you could manage to live.'"

The prisoners moved like sleep walkers, half dead, protected somehow from seeing anything, from feeling anything. "'But Anne had no such protection,'" another survivor recalled. "'I can still see her standing at the door and looking down the camp street as a herd of naked gypsy girls was driven by to the crematory, and Anne watched them go and cried. And she cried also when we marched past the Hungarian children who had already been waiting half a day in the rain in front of the gas chambers because it was not yet their turn. And Anne nudged me and said: "Look, look. Their eyes . . ."'"

In October 1944 Anne, Margot, and Mrs. Van Daan were among a group of the youngest and strongest women selected to be moved to Belsen in Germany. Left alone, refusing to eat, her mind wandering, Mrs. Frank died in the infirmary barracks at Auschwitz on January 6, 1945. Otto Frank, in the men's camp, saw Mr. Van Daan taken off to be gassed. Mr. Dussel was sent back to Germany and died in the Neuengamme camp. When the SS abandoned Auschwitz, in February 1945, to escape the advancing Russians, they took Peter Van Daan with them on the winter march to the west; he was never heard from again. Otto Frank survived to be liberated by the Russians.

Belsen, Anne discovered, was different from Auschwitz. There was no organization, no roll call, no food or water, only the barren, frozen heath and the starving people looking like ghosts. By January 1945 the Allies had reached the Rhine, but at Belsen typhus raged and hope was dead.

At Belsen, Anne found her school friend, Lies Goosens. "'I waited shivering in the darkness,'" Lies related of the night when Anne was brought to her. "'It took a long time. But suddenly I heard a voice: "Lies, Lies? Where are you?"'

"'It was Anne, and I ran in the direction of the voice, and then I saw her beyond the barbed wire. She was in rags. I saw her emaciated, sunken face in the darkness. Her eyes were very large. We cried and cried, for now there was only the barbed wire between us, nothing more. And no longer any difference in our fates.

"'I told Anne that my mother had died and my father was dying, and Anne told me that she knew nothing about her father, but that her mother had stayed behind in Auschwitz. Only Margot was still with her, but she was already very sick. They had met up with Mrs. Van Daan again only after their arrival here in Belsen.'"

Mrs. Van Daan died at Belsen, but no witness marked the date. Margot died at the end of February or beginning of March 1945. "'Anne, who was already sick at the time,'" recalled a survivor, "'was not informed of her sister's death; but after a few days she sensed it, and soon afterwards she died, peacefully, feeling that nothing bad was happening to her.'" She was not yet sixteen.

In May 1945 the war ended. Months later, Otto Frank returned to Amsterdam by way of Odessa and Marseilles. Miep and Elli gave him the notebooks and papers in Anne's handwriting that they had found strewn over the floor of the "secret annex" after the Gestapo had gone. These were Anne's diary, stories, and sketches. They were all that remained.

At first Otto Frank had copies of the diary privately circulated as a memorial to his family. It was a Dutch university professor who urged formal publication of the book, and with only slight excisions by Mr. Frank *Het Achterbuis (The Secret Annex)* was published in Amsterdam by Contact Publishers in June 1947. The book soon went through several editions. In 1950 it was published in Germany by the Heidelberg firm of Lambert Schneider. The first printing was only 4500 copies, and many booksellers were actually afraid to show it in their windows; but the book caught on rapidly, and sales of the pocket edition, published by S. Fischer Verlag, totaled 900,000. In 1950 the diary was published in France; in 1952, in England and the United States under the title *Anne Frank: The Diary of a Young Girl.* Now, twenty years after its original publication, the book has been translated into thirty-one languages, including Bengali, Slovene, and Esperanto. It has been published in thirty countries, and has sold more than one million copies in hard-cover alone. In the United States the diary and *The Works of Anne Frank,* both published by Doubleday & Company, have sold well over 150,000 copies and the Pocket Book edition of the diary has sold almost four million copies. The diary was also distributed by the Teen Age Book Club and the Book Find Club and was reprinted in the Modern Library. It was serialized by an American newspaper syndicate with an estimated audience of ten million readers, and millions more read it when it was condensed in *Omnibook* and *Compact* magazines. A German translation of the book has been used in the United States as a school reader, and a large-type edition has been published by Franklin Watts, Inc.

In 1955 a play by Frances Goodrich and Albert Hackett based on the diary and called simply *The Diary of Anne Frank* opened at the Cort Theatre in New York. A great success, it received the Pulitzer Prize, the Critics Circle Prize, and the Antoinette Perry Award for 1956. On October 1, 1956, *The Diary of Anne Frank* opened simultaneously in seven German cities. Audiences there greeted it in stunned silence. The play released a wave of emotion that finally broke through the silence with which Germans had treated the Nazi period. For the first time there were widespread expressions of guilt and shame for what Germans had done to the Jews only a few years before.

In Amsterdam, Queen Juliana attended the play's opening on November 27. This was the city where the events of the play had actually occurred, and many Netherlanders who had lost families and friends in the extermination of the Dutch Jews were in the audience. "There were audible sobs," the *New York Times* correspondent reported, "and one strangled cry as the drama struck its climax and conclusion—the sound of the Germans hammering at the door of the hideout. The audience sat in silence for several minutes after the curtain went down and then rose as the royal party left. There was no applause."

In the United States, *The Diary of Anne Frank* was made into a motion picture in 1959 and adapted for television in 1967.

But still the story was not finished. With the passing of the years, more and more details of Anne Frank's life became known. In 1958 Ernst Schnabel published his moving book for which he interviewed forty-two people who had known Anne or whose lives had touched hers. In 1963 a Viennese police inspector, Karl Silberbauer, was identified as the Gestapo sergeant who had arrested the Franks in 1944. Silberbauer protested that he had merely followed orders. He was suspended from his post but was later acquitted of the charge of having concealed his past. In January 1966, the Nazi police chief in the Netherlands during World War II, former SS lieutenant general Wilhelm Harster, together with two former aides, was arrested in Munich. The three were charged with having directed the deportation of nearly 100,000 Dutch Jews to Auschwitz. One of their victims had been Anne Frank. At their trial a year later, a former SS major, Wilhelm Zopf, testified that the Franks' betrayer—probably an employee in the warehouse—had received the usual reward of five gulden (about $1.40) for each of the persons taken from the "secret annex." The German court sentenced Harster to fifteen years in prison, his accomplices to nine years and five years.

Anne Frank's wish—"I want to go on living even after my death"—has come true. Today the Anne Frank Foundation maintains the building on the Prinsengracht Canal where the Franks hid for twenty-five months as a memorial to Anne Frank. Each year the house is visited by thousands of people from all over the world. The Foundation is also working toward the future by helping to promote better understanding among young people from every part of the world. To this end it has established the International Youth Center, which serves as a meeting place for young people and which holds lectures, discussions, and conferences covering a wide range of international problems.

The Montessori School in Amsterdam is now the Anne Frank school. There are other memorials to her in Germany, Israel, and elsewhere to atone for the unmarked grave at Belsen. But above all, the diary remains. "Her voice was preserved," Ernst Schnabel wrote, "out of the millions that were silenced, this voice no louder than a child's whisper. . . . It has outlasted the shouts of the murderers and has soared above the voices of time."

If Suddenly You Come for Me

N. Nor

Translated by Keith Bosley

If suddenly you come for me
To throw me in an iron cage
I'll leave the world with head held high
And I shall not repent or rage.
I'll step into the cold abyss
With no appeals, complaints or tears:
Nor shall my Vision be amiss—
Her I have cherished down the years.
And far from friends, between thick walls
We'll live to see the day we're free.
I do not fear your long-term jails.
She dies not, nor can you kill me.

from
Simon Wiesenthal

Hella Pick

A survivor of the death camps, Simon Wiesenthal spent his life pursuing Nazi war criminals and bringing them to justice. His greatest fame came from his contribution to the hunt for Adolf Eichmann (the Nazi who organized and oversaw the details of how to kill all European Jews). Yet there have been many other cases in Wiesenthal's quest that "no Nazi murderer, however old he may be, will be allowed to die in peace." Through the pursuit of this goal, and the publicity it brings, Wiesenthal seeks to educate younger generations about the Holocaust, and to warn "the murderers of tomorrow—who may not even be born yet— . . . that they will have no peace."

In the following excerpt from Wiesenthal's biography, the author shows how Wiesenthal pursued his twin aims of education and justice by tracking down the man who arrested Anne Frank.

IN Holland, where Anne Frank's diary is required school reading, its authenticity always went unquestioned. The same did not apply in Austria and Germany. Wiesenthal first understood the long arm of Holocaust revisionism in 1958, when a performance of a play based on the diary of Anne Frank in Linz was interrupted by anti-Semitic demonstrators, all of them children in their teens, high-school pupils, shouting "swindle" and booing loudly. The Anne Frank story was all a fraud, they remonstrated. A couple of days later, Wiesenthal overheard a conversation, in which a young student expressed regret at having missed the demonstration. The youth went on to argue that there was no evidence to prove that Anne Frank ever lived, and went on to assert that the diary was most likely a forgery. Without proof, it could all be a big lie. "Nobody will believe you unless you find the man who arrested her," one boy challenged Wiesenthal.

Wiesenthal interpreted such remarks as proof that a new generation was being fed lies and deceptions by its teachers and parents anxious to obliterate the past. He had to find the SS man who had arrested Anne Frank and had sent her on to Bergen-Belsen concentration camp, where she had died.

It took him five years. Dutch schoolchildren always listen with rapt attention when he tells them the story of his search. At the start, the only clue he found was in the appendix to the Anne Frank diary, where Paul Kraler, an employee of the Frank family business, records how he had tried to intercede with the Gestapo after the Franks' arrest. He failed, but mentioned that he had spoken with the officer who had made the arrests. He was, Kraler said, an Austrian SS man, the first half of whose name was "Silver." That could not have been right since Silver is an English word, unlikely to occur in a German-speaking country. But perhaps, Wiesenthal reasoned, the policeman's name had been a combination of "Silber," a common enough name in Austria. Wiesenthal checked through the people of that name listed in the Vienna telephone directory and in the directories of some of the Austrian provinces. It was like looking for a needle in a haystack. He was able to identify eight "Silbernagels," who had been members of the Nazi Party or of the SS, but none fitted the policeman's profile.

Wiesenthal says that he was tempted to contact Otto Frank, Anne's father, who had survived and was living in Basle, but he was clearly afraid of being accused of unwarranted interference in private grief. Mr. Frank had already declared his readiness to forgive and his desire for reconciliation. Wiesenthal, who opposed forgiveness and wanted the guilty punished, feared that Mr. Frank might urge him to give up the hunt for the arresting officer.

During a visit to Amsterdam in 1963, Wiesenthal talked about the continuing search for various prominent members of the Gestapo in Holland during the war, and as a parting present one of his new Dutch friends gave him some reading material for his return flight, a copy of a 1943 directory of SS personnel in Holland. When the plane took off, Wiesenthal scanned the names. It was a soporific, and he became sleepy. But suddenly he sat up, startled. His eyes had lit upon a page headed "IVb 4 *Joden* [Jews]." It listed the personnel involved in rounding up Jews. There were four names including that of "Silberbauer." That had to be his man, but where was he now? There were numerous Silberbauers in the Vienna telephone directory alone. Even the textile shop on the Rudolfsplatz was called Silberbauer.

Wiesenthal asked for help from a friendly Austrian Ministry of the Interior official, Dr. Josef Wiesinger. The Ministry soon iden-

tified the man, who was now an inspector in Vienna's police
force. Silberbauer was suspended from his duties. But acting on
instructions from senior Interior Ministry quarters, where
Wiesenthal's activism had become anathema, Wiesenthal was
kept in ignorance. The first he heard about Silberbauer's sus-
pension came from the Austrian Communist Party's newspaper,
the *Volksstimme*, which claimed a scoop with a story that Karl
Silberbauer had been suspended, pending investigation and
possible prosecution for his role in the arrest of Anne Frank.
Moscow radio and the Soviet party paper *Izvestia* followed up
with claims that Austria's resistance fighters and "vigilant comrades" had uncovered Anne Frank's captor. Wiesenthal was
angry: the Interior Ministry had kept bad faith with him, to put
it at its mildest. He would repay in kind. He invited a friendly
Dutch journalist and recounted how he had traced Silberbauer's identity. The story was given great prominence around
the world. Anne Frank's father does not appear to have appreci-
ated Wiesenthal's intrusion. Otto Frank reacted to the publicity
with the assertion that he had long known his daughter had
been arrested by a policeman called Silberbauer. Wiesenthal
has always doubted that Frank was being truthful. He remarks
scathingly that Anne's father rebuffed suggestions that the man
should be prosecuted by using the classic apologia that Silberbauer had only done his duty.

This was also the excuse adopted by Silberbauer himself, and
by the Austrian authorities who decided that the arrest of Anne
Frank did not warrant Silberbauer's prosecution as a war criminal, because there was no evidence that he had also been responsible for her deportation. Wiesenthal thought that perhaps
he could raise the stakes by building up popular pressure to in-
sist on a trial. He called another press conference. Next day he
looked for headlines in the Austrian press, but for once there
were none. A far more important event had occurred: President
Kennedy's assassination.

In Wiesenthal's report on the activities of the Documentation
Center during the second half of 1963, he gave top billing to the
endeavors to unmask the man who had arrested Anne Frank.
He wrote that the search must continue for more evidence to
make out a viable case against Silberbauer. There was always a
chance that a reader might have incriminating information. Apparently none was found, and Wiesenthal accepted that there
was no alternative but to abandon the campaign for Silberbauer's prosecution. At least, he felt, his principal objective had

been met: the man had been found and the world now had living proof of Anne's arrest. The authenticity of her diary was secure. Wiesenthal was satisfied that at last "the neo-Nazis stopped questioning the authenticity of her diary to support their denial of the Holocaust."

However, in *The Murderers Amongst Us*, Wiesenthal hints at his frustration that Silberbauer was never held to account before the law: "Of course, he doesn't matter at all. Compared to other names on my list, he is a nobody, a zero. But the figure before the zero was Anne Frank."

Three Poems

Hannah Senesh

Hannah Senesh escaped to Palestine (which later became the state of Israel after World War II) before the Nazi persecution of Hungarian Jews began. There she put off her dreams of becoming a writer and did the work needed to build the Jewish nation she dreamed about.

When news reached Palestine of the terrible persecution the Nazis were inflicting upon the Jews of Europe, Hannah again put her life on hold and volunteered to parachute behind enemy lines into Hungary. There her mission was to disrupt Nazi operations and to help Jewish refugees and British airmen out of the country. She was captured and executed in prison at the age of twenty-three.

The first two poems were written during her time with the partisans, fighting against the Nazis and hoping for a better world. The last poem, "Blessed Is the Match," was given to a friend just before Hannah crossed the Hungarian border and was captured.

We gathered flowers in the fields and mountains,
We breathed the fresh winds of spring,
We were drenched with the warmth of the sun's rays
In our Homeland, in our beloved home.

We go out to our brothers in exile,
To the suffering of winter, to frost in the night.
Our hearts will bring tidings of springtime
Our lips sing the song of light.

You are not alone. Here is your sea.
The sand, the shore, the sea, the waves,
The dreams, the hopes that brought you here.

They waited for your coming. They stayed;
The sand, the shore, the sea, the waves,
They knew: the black night would bring you here.

And the myriad eyes in the sky
Wink into your two from on high
Stealing from the endless sea—a tear.

• • •

Blessed Is the Match

Blessed is the match consumed
in kindling flame.

Blessed is the flame that burns
in the secret fastness of the heart.

Blessed is the heart with strength to stop
its beating for honor's sake.

Blessed is the match consumed
in kindling flame.

The Warsaw Ghetto Uprising

Deborah Bachrach

Once the Jews of Europe understood there could be no compromise with the Nazis, pockets of resistance formed. Jewish partisan groups engaged in guerrilla tactics, disrupting the German war effort any way they could. From Palestine, a small number of volunteers parachuted into German-held territory to help their fellow Jews. In Sobibor, a Nazi death camp, hundreds of Jewish inmates managed to kill several of their guards and flee into the nearby woods. Yet for all the courage shown in those acts of rebellion, the best known defiance to the Nazis was the Warsaw Ghetto Uprising.

WITHOUT warning, on January 18, 1943, German troops surrounded the ghetto. Their immediate orders were to gather up eight thousand Jews during the next few days. The resistance fighters, caught unprepared, could not mount a general defense. Instead, individual groups from the Jewish resistance jumped into action.

A handful of young men, for example, mingled with the slowly moving crowds of Jews who responded to the German order to assemble at the deportation center. When the Jews approached the corners of Zamenhof and Niska Streets toward the *Umschlagplatz*, the resistance fighters fired at German soldiers, engaged in hand-to-hand combat, and screamed at the assembled Jews to disperse and hide. Most of the members of this small resistance group were killed that day but they had taken the first overt step against the German enemy.

The Germans were stunned. The Jews had never openly resisted the German army. No German had ever fallen in battle with a Jew.

During the January *Aktion* the Germans succeeded in rounding up about five thousand Jews, four thousand on the first day. The remaining Jews of the Warsaw ghetto went into hiding, resisting the efforts of the Germans to murder them. Another thousand Jews were forcibly dragged from buildings. The January *Aktion* ended after four days. The Germans had failed to round up their quota of Jews.

The Jews remaining in the ghetto underwent a great psychological change. They realized that passively obeying German orders would gain them nothing. The remaining people in the ghetto embraced the Z.O.B.'s attitudes and methods. The Z.O.B. came to "assume responsibility for the fate of the entire community."

For the first time nonfighters refused to respond to the imperious German commands to appear at the *Umschlagplatz* for deportation. Instead, they demonstrated defiant passive resistance. The Warsaw ghetto uprising was the only case during World War II in which the resistance fighters had the active and continuing support of the community for which they fought.

The Jewish nonfighters began to dig themselves into bunkers. Several groups of people got together and designed very elaborate underground hiding places complete with food supplies, connections to existing water systems, and physician members. The bunkers were disguised so well that the entrances were almost invisible. Many people in the bunkers still hoped that they would find a way to survive.

The resistance fighters of the Z.O.B. knew better. They did not build themselves bunkers, but lived in temporary shelters because their strategy called for sudden movement at short notice. They made no plans for escape.

Between January and April 1943 fewer than a thousand young men and women fighters stepped up their military training for the inevitable return of the Germans. They drilled, they prepared positions, they kept constant lookouts posted near each of the ghetto entrances, and they made every effort to build up their very limited arsenal.

Warsaw Uprising

ON April 18, 1943, the Germans returned to the Warsaw ghetto. Two thousand Lithuanian, Ukrainian, and SS troops, heavily armed, wearing body protection and supported by tanks, appeared at the main entrance of the ghetto. The Jews were nowhere to be seen. Cautiously the Germans and their tanks entered the ghetto. Gunfire erupted. One tank was hit by Jewish light arms and put out of action. Under attack at several points, the German force retreated. Haim Frymer, a Jewish fighter, wrote, "We heard the astonished outcry of the Germans, *Juden haven Waffen, Juden haven Waffen* [the Jews have arms]."

Hitler dismissed von Sammern-Frankenegg for failing to alert him to the possibility of an armed uprising by the Jews. He was replaced by SS general Jurgen Stroop. Stroop kept a diary of the uprising, recording his impressions of the fighting, which extended to the middle of May.

The German troops returned to the ghetto day after day. While the passive resisters kept themselves hidden within their bunkers, the Z.O.B. fired on the Germans from rooftops and building windows. Battles were fierce but brief. The resistance fighters had few weapons and had to make each shot or homemade bomb count.

The Germans had at first expected to wipe out the resistance within a few days and deport the remaining Jews immediately thereafter. Instead the battle for the Warsaw ghetto continued. Stroop discovered the makeshift ladders that allowed the Jews to move from building to building. He had his troops block the passages in the roofs and building attics where the ladders had rested.

He attached listening devices near the basement entrances of buildings to see if his troops could discover the location of underground bunkers. He brought in dogs to sniff out underground hiding places and piles of rubble where survivors might have found space in which to conceal themselves. The Germans were taken completely by surprise by the existence of the bunkers. Stroop made the following entry in his diary:

> The number of Jews taken from their houses in the ghetto during the first days was too slight. It turns out that the Jews hid in the sewerage canals and bunkers that were prepared especially for that purpose. During the first days, it was assumed that there were merely a few isolated bunkers, but in the course of the great action it became clear that the entire ghetto is systematically provided with cellars, bunkers and passageways. Each of these passageways and bunkers has an outlet to the sewerage canals. Hence, this allowed for the undisturbed underground contact. This effective network also served the Jews as a means of escaping to the "Aryan" side of Warsaw. We received constant reports that the Jews were trying to escape through the underground canals."

The Germans began to set fire to the ghetto systematically, house by house, day by day. The fires destroyed the buildings, sucked the air from the bunkers, and severed the water connections that the Jews had created earlier in preparation for the uprising.

The fire and smoke of the burning ghetto could be seen for miles around. Men, women, and children were incinerated in the blaze. Those who survived long enough to stumble out of their bunkers were shot by the Germans. It is reported that not a single bunker was taken intact by the Germans during the uprising.

On April 25, Stroop sent a message to his superiors: "If last night what was the ghetto was alight and burning, tonight it is one mighty furnace." But several days later he had to report that "Repeatedly we saw that the Jews and bandits preferred to go back into the fire than to fall into our hands."

Each day resistance to the Germans diminished as the Jewish fighters fell in battle. Each day, the area still under their control contracted. Those few who survived regrouped, each day finding resistance more difficult to sustain.

Finally, on May 8, 1943, the Germans located the center of the Z.O.B. on 18 Mila Street. The Germans closed all entrances to the position and injected poison gas and threw hand grenades into the underground space. . . .

Destroying the Ghetto

ON May 16, 1943, German forces destroyed the main synagogue of the Warsaw ghetto. General Stroop wrote in his diary: "The former Jewish Quarter of Warsaw no longer exists. According to our evidence, the total number of Jews seized and terminated is 50,065."

The Warsaw ghetto uprising ended. No buildings stood intact. Almost all the passive resisters had died in their bunkers or had been killed as they attempted to escape. Most of the fighters were dead. However, for months after, individuals continued to emerge from the ruins of Warsaw.

A handful of resistance fighters, perhaps seventy-five survivors, made their way through the sewers that ran under the ghetto to the area beyond the ghetto walls. Some were killed as they emerged from the sewers. The Germans sprayed bullets at those resistance fighters who had not yet emerged from the sewers. Some actually managed to escape.

So the Warsaw ghetto, home at one time between 1939 and 1943 to well over half a million Jews, ceased to exist. What could not be destroyed, however, was the memory of the uprising itself.

In the words of historian Isaac Kowalski, the resistance had gained a "moral victory of death in battle, rather than in the gas chambers."

According to Kowalski, "The revolt was conceived on a moral plain; a battle for the honor of their people, for the future of their people. It was an act that grew out of the great yearning for human dignity." The handful of young Jewish resistance fighters dispelled the idea that Jews do not fight. News of the uprising spread throughout Europe and gave hope to many others who tried to resist German efforts to murder them. The myth of the indestructibility of the German army suffered a severe blow as a result of the uprising. Many Jews regarded the uprising with honor and held it in the same regard as the heroic battles fought by Jewish bands against Roman legions so many centuries before.

from
Righteous Gentile

John Bierman

By 1944 the United States could no longer ignore the evidence of the Nazis' atrocities toward the Jews. Realizing they had to act immediately to prevent the murder of 750,000 Jews in Hungary, the U.S. asked neutral Sweden to send an ambassador to save as many of the Hungarian Jews as possible. Sweden agreed, and sent Raoul Wallenberg.

YAD VASHEM, the Martyrs' and Heroes' Remembrance Authority—a complex of buildings, gardens, avenues, and piazzas on a flat hilltop on the western outskirts of Jerusalem—was established by Act of Parliament of the State of Israel in 1953 to commemorate the 6 million Jewish victims of the Nazi Holocaust. It is at once a memorial, museum library, and archive, and a center for study and research into one of history's most terrifying and inexplicable recent phenomena: the attempted destruction of an entire people by an apparently civilized nation. . . .

One of the features of Yad Vashem is an avenue of long-living, evergreen carob trees through which one walks to reach the Holocaust Museum and the stark piazza which commemorates the heroism and martyrdom of the Warsaw ghetto uprising.

This is called the Allée des Justes, the Avenue of the Righteous, and each tree in it has been planted to commemorate a Gentile who risked his or her life to save a Jew or Jews from death during the Hitler years. At the time of writing, some six hundred trees have already been planted in the avenue and in an "overflow" area of terraced hillside beyond the piazza. Two thousand more cases are awaiting consideration by a special committee that is headed by an Israeli Supreme Court justice. This committee's function is to study written and oral evidence about all individuals, many of them now dead, who may qualify for the title of "Righteous Gentile." In each confirmed case, a tree will be planted in the name of the individual concerned and a medal and certificate presented to him or his representative. The medal bears a Talmudic inscription: "Whoever saves a single soul, it is as if he had saved the whole world."

If the Jewish people's accusation that the world stood by and did nothing while they were slaughtered is substantially true—certainly as far as governments and organizations were concerned—those six hundred carob trees, and the many hundreds more that will join them on their sunlit hilltop, are a reminder that individuals can rise above the regimes which represent them and that compassion and courage may be more common qualities among "ordinary" people than the dismal record of "world leaders" allows us to believe. It should not be forgotten that the Nazis' punishment for those who helped Jews was generally that they, and often their families, should suffer a similar fate.

Though marked only by a small plaque bearing the name and nationality of the honored individual, every tree has its story in the Yad Vashem archives.

Those trees speak for all those who, as a former Speaker of Israel's Parliament has put it, "saved not only the Jews but the honor of Man." Of none is this more true than of a relatively unknown Swede, Raoul Wallenberg. Although the authorities of Yad Vashem establish no order of precedence they will readily concede that, without question, he is first among the righteous.

Attorney Gideon Hausner, chairman of Yad Vashem and the man who prosecuted Adolf Eichmann, expresses the special significance of Raoul Wallenberg:

"Here is a man who had the choice of remaining in secure, neutral Sweden when Nazism was ruling Europe. Instead, he left this haven and went to what was then one of the most perilous places in Europe, Hungary. And for what? To save Jews.

"He won his battle and I feel that in this age when there is so little to believe in—so very little on which our young people can pin their hopes and ideals—he is a person to show to the world, which knows so little about him. That is why I believe the story of Raoul Wallenberg should be told and his figure, in all its true proportions, projected into human minds."

. . .

The role Wallenberg played is movingly revealed in the account of Tommy Lapid, now director-general of the Israeli Broadcasting Authority in Jerusalem. In 1944 he was thirteen years old and one of nine hundred people crowded fifteen or twenty to a room in a Swedish-protected house.

"We were hungry, thirsty, and frightened all the time and we were more afraid of the Arrow Cross than of the British, American, and Russian bombardments put together. Those people had guns and they thought the least they could do for the war effort was to kill a few Jews before the Russians got there, so they were entering these houses, which were undefended, and carrying people away. We were very close to the Danube and we heard them shooting people into the river all night.

"I sometimes think that the greatest achievement of the Nazis was that we just accepted the fact that we were destined to be killed. My father was in Mauthausen concentration camp and perished there. I, an only child, stayed with my mother. I kept asking her for bread. I was so hungry. (Years later, if there was no bread in the house, she would get out of bed at night and go down to a café and ask for two slices of bread—although then a very well-to-do lady in Tel Aviv, she had to have some bread in the house because of those days when she couldn't supply me with any.)

"One morning, a group of these Hungarian Fascists came into the house and said all the able-bodied women must go with them. We knew what this meant. My mother kissed me and I cried and she cried. We knew we were parting forever and she left me there, an orphan to all intents and purposes. Then, two or three hours later, to my amazement, my mother returned with the other women. It seemed like a mirage, a miracle. My mother was there—she was alive and she was hugging me and kissing me, and she said one word: 'Wallenberg.'

"I knew who she meant because Wallenberg was a legend among the Jews. In the complete and total hell in which we lived, there was a savior-angel somewhere, moving around. After she had composed herself, my mother told me that they were being taken to the river when a car arrived and out stepped Wallenberg—and they knew immediately who it was, because there was only one such person in the world. He went up to the Arrow Cross leader and protested that the women were under his protection. They argued with him, but he must have had incredible charisma, some great personal authority, because there was absolutely nothing behind him, nothing to back him up. He stood out there in the street, probably feeling the loneliest man in the world, trying to pretend there was something behind him. They could have shot him there and then in the street and nobody would have known about it. Instead, they relented and let the women go."

Time and again, as in the testimony of Joni Moser, Wallenberg's extraordinary personal authority and lonely courage comes through.

"I was Wallenberg's errand boy. As I spoke German as well as Hungarian I could pass through barriers and therefore was well

equipped to be a messenger. I had been served with a deportation order by the Germans but had escaped, and I used to show
the deportation order, embellished with the swastika, to young
Arrow Cross men who could not read German. They only saw
the swastika and let me pass. I always took care to avoid the
Germans but they caught me once, and it was almost the end
for me. But just then Wallenberg happened to come by in his
grand diplomatic car. He stopped and asked me to step forward
for questioning. 'Jump in, quick,' he said—and before the astonished soldiers realized what had happened we were gone. Wallenberg was fantastic! His conduct, his power of organization,
his speed in decision and action! What a strategist! Wallenberg
was the initiator of the whole rescue action, remember that."

Moser recalls the day when Wallenberg learned that eight
hundred Jewish labor service men were being marched to Mauthausen. He and Wallenberg drove to the frontier and caught up
with the column. Wallenberg asked that those with Swedish protective passports should raise their hands. "On his order," Moser
says, "I ran between the ranks and told the men to raise their
hands, whether they had a passport or not. He then claimed cus-
tody of all who had raised their hands and such was his bearing
that none of the Hungarian guards opposed him. The extraordinary thing was the absolutely convincing power of his behavior."

Moser feels that Wallenberg was supremely happy during the
brief period of his most intense activity. "It is not given to many
men to live such a life, equipped with the spark of initiative, an
irresistible personal radiance, and a tireless energy, and with
these to be able to save thousands of one's fellow-men."

Sándor Ardai was sent by the Jewish underground to drive
for Wallenberg after his personal driver, Vilmos Langfelder, was
arrested by the Arrow Cross on 7 November. Ardai's first impression was that Wallenberg didn't look at all like a hero—"he
seemed rather dreamy and soft." Ardai's first mission was to
drive Wallenberg to Arrow Cross headquarters on 9 November
and wait outside "until he had got Langfelder back.

"As he vanished with long strides into the Arrow Cross headquarters I thought to myself, He'll never do it. How was it possible that the Arrow Cross would release a prisoner just because
one man demanded it? But when I saw him come back down the
stairs he had Langfelder with him. They jumped into the car and
I drove them straight to the legation. Nobody commented on
what had happened and I began to understand the extraordinary
power that was in Raoul Wallenberg.

"During the month and a half that Langfelder and I took turns to drive him I never heard him speak an unnecessary word, never a superfluous comment or a word of complaint, even though he often had only a few hours' sleep over several days. Only once I saw him upset. It was when an Arrow Cross gang had occupied his office. He asked the government, without success, to have it returned. Then he led a small group of us straight back to the office and threw out the intruders. Once that was done, he sat down at his desk. We felt sure that there would be reprisals, but astonishingly nothing happened."

Ardai tells how, one day in November, he drove Wallenberg to the Józsefváros Railway Station, where Wallenberg had learned that a trainload of Jews was about to leave for Auschwitz. The young SS officer supervising the transport ordered Wallenberg off the platform. Wallenberg brushed past him.

"Then he climbed up on the roof of the train and began handing in protective passes through the doors which were not yet sealed. He ignored orders from the Germans for him to get down, then the Arrow Cross men began shooting and shouting at him to go away. He ignored them and calmly continued handing out passports to the hands that were reaching out for them. I believe the Arrow Cross men deliberately aimed over his head, as not one shot hit him, which would have been impossible otherwise. I think this is what they did because they were so impressed by his courage.

"After Wallenberg had handed over the last of the passports he ordered all those who had one to leave the train and walk to a caravan of cars parked nearby, all marked in Swedish colors. I don't remember exactly how many, but he saved dozens off that train, and the Germans and Arrow Cross were so dumbfounded they let him get away with it!"

There are many eyewitness accounts of Wallenberg facing down German and Hungarian officers in this way. With the Germans, especially, his technique was to pull rank. "How dare you attempt to remove these people who are under the protection of the Royal Swedish legation?" he once berated a young Nazi lieutenant in charge of a transport of Jews. "Don't you realize that your government relies on my Foreign Ministry to protect its interests in many of the most important countries of the world? And this is how you protect our interests! Wait until word of this affair reaches your superiors. I shall complain direct to Berlin. I shall have your head on a platter!"

"But I have my orders," replied the flustered lieutenant. "All the Jews on this list are to be transported."

"Your list cannot possibly include Jews who hold Swedish passports," snapped Wallenberg. "And if it does then someone has made a grievous mistake that he will pay for." Then he produced a list of his own, which he brandished in front of the intimidated young Nazi. In the end, he got "his" Jews off the train.

There were times when Wallenberg elevated bluff to a fine art, such as the occasion when he got a group of Jewish deportees to win their freedom by producing all kinds of official-looking but irrelevant documents—like driving licenses and tax receipts—which he showed to a German officer as evidence of their protected status, banking successfully on the likelihood that the Nazi could not read a word of Hungarian.

Using his well-tried methods of bribery, coercion, and occasionally outright blackmail, Wallenberg was able to build up an impressive private intelligence network that gave him lightning information about deportations, raids on protected houses, and new official anti-Jewish measures. Time after time he was able to turn up—often alone, except for his driver, always unarmed—in time to make a decisive intervention. Once, during the round-up of Jewish men for forced labor, Wallenberg went to a Swedish-protected house which had been forcibly entered by a detachment of Hungarian gendarmes. "This is Swedish territory," he told the officer in charge coldly. "You have no right to be on these premises." The officer replied that he had orders to take all the able-bodied men. "Nonsense," replied Wallenberg. "By agreement between the Royal Swedish government and the Royal Hungarian government, these men are specifically exempted from labor service."

The Hungarian, though obviously discomfited by this calculated reference to not one but two "royal governments," nevertheless insisted. "I have my orders," he said. "I must take them." Wallenberg played his last card: "If you want to take them you will have to shoot me first." The officer faltered and gave in. He and his men left empty-handed. . . .

Wallenberg's inventiveness was apparently as boundless as his energy. At a time when the Arrow Cross were attacking protected houses with alarming frequency he thought of a truly original deterrent. Barna Yaron, twenty-two years old and an escapee from a forced labor battalion, was living with his young bride, Judith, in a "Wallenberg house" in Tatra Street, close to the river.

"Late one night," he says, "I received a message asking me to go down to the street where Wallenberg was waiting in his car to see me. Wondering what he might want, I went down. As we sat together in the back of the car he told me he had hit on the idea of starting rumors of a typhus epidemic in the Swedish houses as a ruse to keep the Arrow Cross gangs from daring to enter. But to make it convincing, he said he needed a 'genuine' typhus case to report to the city health authorities. Would I be it? I was mystified until he went on to explain that he wanted a volunteer to have an injection that would produce what would look like the symptoms of typhus. Well, I was young and strong in those days, and considered myself something of a daredevil, so I said 'What the . . .' and agreed, but I can tell you I was really scared. Anyway, we went along to the Jewish clinic for me to get my injection, but it seems that the doctor concerned got cold feet and decided that it really was too dangerous and he might start a real epidemic. So the whole idea was called off, but you can see how Wallenberg's mind was working all the time."

Wallenberg never forgot the importance of paperwork. He bombarded the Hungarian Foreign Ministry with protest notes every time he had evidence of the violation of a protective pass or the unauthorized entry of a protected house. Since such infringements were happening all the time he was sometimes sending two protests a day to the Foreign Ministry. In the first half of November he sent twenty. They had their effect. Ministry officials, worn down by this relentless paper assault, would plead with police, gendarmerie, and Arrow Cross officials to leave the Swedish-protected Jews alone.

Thanks to Wallenberg, it was even possible for some of the Jews to find something to laugh at in this situation. Edit Ernster recalls this grim humor: "It seems so strange, this country of super-Aryans—the Swedes—taking us under their wing. Often, when an Orthdox Jew went by, in his hat, beard, and sidelocks, we'd say: 'Look, there goes another Swede.'"

Overworked as he was, and concerned with the fate of thousands, Wallenberg nevertheless found time for acts of individual kindness. All hospitals were barred to Jews and conditions in the houses were atrociously overcrowded and insanitary. When Wallenberg heard that the wife of Tibor Vándor, a young Jew who was working on his C Section staff in a legation office in Tigris Street, was about to have a baby, he swiftly rounded up a doctor, taking him and the young couple to his flat in Ostrom Street. There, he turned his own bed over to Agnes, the young mother-to-be, and went out into the corridor to sleep. In the small hours of the morning he was awakened by the doctor, who told him that Agnes Vándor had given birth to a healthy baby girl. Wallenberg went in to inspect the new arrival and the

Vándors begged him to be her godfather. He consented happily and the child was named Yvonne Maria Eva.

During the final days of the European struggle—when Soviet forces were closing in on Hungary, and the Germans were retreating—the Nazis planned a mass evacuation of the remaining Jewish ghettos. The Germans' intent was to march the Jews to Germany, where they would all be killed. Thankfully, Raoul Wallenberg learned of this plan in time. Sending a representative to the Nazi general in charge (Wallenberg dared not go himself, lest the Germans shoot him), the Swedish ambassador warned the general he would be hanged as a war criminal if the deportations took place. Having no time to hunt for Wallenberg and silence him, the general ordered the operation canceled. Wallenberg's quick thinking and decisive action in this matter alone saved close to one hundred thousand lives.

Fate would not prove kind to Raoul Wallenberg. When the Germans and the other ambassadors fled before the approaching Soviet army, Wallenberg stayed in Hungary in order to arrange for food and medical supplies for the suffering Jewish community. Unfortunately, the Soviets did not believe his humanitarian motivations and arrested Wallenberg as a spy. He was thrown into prison where, more than fifty years after the war, he has probably died.

from
Schindler's List

Thomas Keneally

At the risk of his own life, German industrialist Oskar Schindler saved more than a thousand Jews from the death camps. After the war, Israel would recognize his bravery by awarding him the title of a Righteous Person, granting him a plaque in the Park of Heroes, and inviting him to plant a tree on the Avenue of the Righteous. Later, Germany would also recognize Schindler's heroism by granting him the Cross of Merit, and a small pension (to make up for the fortune he lost because of the war).

The following excerpt takes place shortly after Germany's conquest of Poland—before Oskar Schindler became aware of the Nazis' plans for the Jews.

IN late October 1939, two young German NCOs entered the showroom of J. C. Buchheister & Company in Stradom Street, Cracow, and insisted on buying some expensive bolts of cloth to send home. The Jewish clerk behind the counter, a yellow star sewn to his breast, explained that Buchheister's did not sell direct to the public but supplied garment factories and retail outlets. The soldiers would not be dissuaded. When it was time to settle their bill, they did it whimsically with a Bavarian banknote of 1858 and a piece of German Army Occupation scrip dated 1914. "Perfectly good currency," one of them told the Jewish bookkeeper. They were healthy-looking young men who had spent all spring and summer on maneuvers, the early autumn yielding them an easy triumph and, later, all the latitude of conquerors in a sweet city. The bookkeeper agreed to the transaction and got them out of the shop before ringing up a sale on the cash register.

Later in the day, a young German accounts manager, an official appointed by the deftly named East Trust Agency to take over and run Jewish businesses, visited the showroom. He was one of two German officials assigned to Buchheister. The first was Sepp Aue, the supervisor, a middle-aged, unambitious man, and the second, this young go-getter. The young man inspected the books and the till. He took out the valueless currency. What did it mean, this comic-opera money?

The Jewish bookkeeper told his story; the accounts manager accused him of substituting the antique notes for the hard złoty. Later in the day, in Buchheister's warehouse upstairs, the go-getter reported to Sepp Aue and said they should call in the *Schutzpolizei.*

Herr Aue and the young accountant both knew that such an act would lead to the imprisonment of the bookkeeper in the SS jail in Montelupich Street. The accountant thought that this would set an excellent example for Buchheister's remaining Jewish staff. But the idea distressed Aue, who had a secret lia-bility of his own, his grandmother having been Jewish, though no one had yet found that out.

Aue sent an office boy with a message to the company's origi-nal accountant, a Polish Jew named Itzhak Stern, who was at home with influenza. Aue was a political appointee with little accounting experience. He wanted Stern to come into the office and resolve the impasse over the bolts of linen. He had just sent the message off to Stern's house in Podgórze when his secretary came into the office and announced that a Herr Oskar Schindler was waiting outside, claiming to have an appointment. Aue went into the outer room and saw a tall young man, placid as a large dog, tranquilly smoking. The two had met at a party the night before. Oskar had been there with a Sudeten German girl named Ingrid, *Treuhänder,* or supervisor, of a Jewish hardware company, just as Aue was *Treuhänder* of Buchheister's. They were a glamorous couple, Oskar and this Ingrid, frankly in love, stylish, with lots of friends in the *Abwehr.*

Herr Schindler was looking for a career in Cracow. Textiles? Aue had suggested. "It isn't just uniforms. The Polish domestic market itself is large enough and inflated enough to support us all. You're welcome to look Buchheister's over," he'd urged Oskar, not knowing how he might regret his tipsy camaraderie at 2 P.M. the next day.

Schindler could see that Herr Aue had possible second thoughts about his invitation. If it's not convenient *Herr Treuhänder,* Oskar suggested . . .

Herr Aue said not at all and took Schindler through the ware-house and across a yard to the spinning division, where great rolls of golden fabric were running off the machines. Schindler asked if the *Treuhänder* had had trouble with the Poles. No, said Sepp, they're cooperative. Stunned, if anything. After all, it's not exactly a munitions factory.

Schindler so obviously had the air of a man with connections that Aue could not resist the temptation to test the point. Did Oskar know the people at the Main Armaments Board? Did he know General Julius Schindler, for example. Perhaps General Schindler was a relative.

That makes no difference, said Herr Schindler disarmingly. (In fact General Schindler was unrelated to him.) The General wasn't such a bad fellow, compared with some, said Oskar.

Aue agreed. But he himself would never dine with General Schindler or meet him for drinks; that was the difference.

They returned to the office, encountering on the way Itzhak Stern, Buchheister's Jewish accountant, waiting on a chair provided by Aue's secretary, blowing his nose and coughing harshly. He stood up, joined his hands one on top of the other in front of his chest, and with immense eyes watched both conquerors approach, pass him, and enter the office. There Aue offered Schindler a drink and then, excusing himself, left Oskar by the fire and went out to interview Stern.

He was so thin, and there was a scholarly dryness to him. He had the manners of a Talmudic scholar, but also of a European intellectual. Aue told him the story of the bookkeeper and the NCOs and the assumptions the young German accountant had made. He produced from the safe the currency: the 1858 Bavarian, the 1914 Occupation. "I thought you might have instituted an accounting procedure to deal with just this situation," said Aue. "It must be happening a great deal in Cracow just now."

Itzhak Stern took the notes and studied them. He had indeed developed a procedure, he told the *Herr Treuhänder*. Without a smile or a wink, he moved to the open fire at the end of the room and dropped both notes into it.

"I write these transactions off to profit and loss, under 'free samples,'" he said. There had been a lot of free samples since September.

Aue liked Stern's dry, effective style with the legal evidence. He began to laugh, seeing in the accountant's lean features the complexities of Cracow itself, the parochial canniness of a small city. Only a local knew the ropes. In the inner office Herr Schindler sat in need of local information.

Aue led Stern through into the manager's office to meet Herr Schindler, who stood staring at the fire. . . . The first thing Itzak

Stern thought was, *This isn't a manageable German.* Aue wore the badge of his *Führer,* a miniature *Hakenkreuz,* as negligently as a man might wear the badge of a cycling club. But big Schindler's coin-sized emblem took the light from the fire in its black enamel. It, and the young man's general affluence, were all the more the symbols of Stern's autumn griefs as a Polish Jew with a cold.

Aue made the introductions. According to the edict already issued by Governor Frank, Stern made his statement: "I have to tell you, sir, that I am a Jew."

"Well," Herr Schindler growled at him. "I'm a German. So there we are!"

All very well, Stern almost intoned privately behind his sodden handkerchief. *In that case, lift the edict.*

For Itzhak Stern was a man—even now, in only the seventh week of the New Order in Poland—not under one edict but already under many. Hans Frank, Governor General of Poland, had already initiated and signed six restrictive edicts, leaving others to his district governor, Dr. Otto Wächter, an SS *Gruppenführer* (equivalent to major general), to implement. Stern, besides declaring his origins, had also to carry a distinctive registration card marked by a yellow stripe. The Orders-in-Council forbidding kosher preparation of meats and commanding forced labor for Jews were three weeks old when Stern stood coughing in Schindler's presence. And Stern's official ration as an *Untermensch* (subhuman) was little more than half that of a non-Jewish Pole, the latter being tainted by *Untermensch*-hood himself.

Finally, by an edict of November 8, a general registration of all Cracovian Jews had begun and was required to be completed by the 24th.

Stern, with his calm and abstract cast of mind, knew that the edicts would continue, would circumscribe his living and breathing further still. Most Cracow Jews expected such a rash of edicts. There would be some disruption of life—Jews from the *shtetls* being brought to town to shovel coal, intellectuals being sent into the countryside to hoe beets. There would also be sporadic slaughters for a time, like the one over at Tursk where an SS artillery unit had kept people working on a bridge all day and then driven them into the village synagogue in the evening and shot them. There would always be such intermittent instances. But the situation would settle; the race would survive by petitioning, by buying off the authorities—it was the old method, it had been working since the Roman Empire, it would work again. In the end the civil authorities needed Jews, especially in a nation where they were one in every eleven.

Stern, however, wasn't one of the sanguine ones. He didn't presume that the legislation would soon achieve a plateau of negotiable severity. For these were the worst of times. So though he did not know that the coming fire would be different in substance as well as degree, he was already resentful enough of the future to think, *All very well for you, Herr Schindler, to make generous little gestures of equality.*

This man, said Aue, introducing Itzhak Stern, was Buchheister's right-hand man. He had good connections in the business community here in Cracow.

It was not Stern's place to argue with Aue about that. Even so, he wondered if the *Treuhänder* wasn't gilding the lily for the distinguished visitor.

Aue excused himself.

Left alone with Stern, Schindler murmured that he'd be grateful if the accountant could tell him what he knew about some of the local businesses. Testing Oskar, Stern suggested that perhaps Herr Schindler should speak to the officials of the Trust Agency.

"They're thieves," said Herr Schindler genially. "They're bureaucrats too. I would like some latitude." He shrugged. "I am a capitalist by temperament and I don't like being regulated."

So Stern and the self-declared capitalist began to talk. And Stern was quite a source; he seemed to have friends or relatives in every factory in Cracow—textiles, garments, confectionery, cabinetmaking, metalwork. Herr Schindler was impressed and took an envelope from the breast pocket of his suit. "Do you know a company called Rekord?" he asked.

Itzhak Stern did. It was in bankruptcy, he said. It had made enamelware. Since it had gone bankrupt some of the metal-press machinery had been confiscated, and now it was largely a shell, producing—under the management of one of the former owners' relatives—a mere fraction of its capacity. His own brother, said Stern, represented a Swiss company that was one of Rekord's major creditors. Stern knew that it was permitted to reveal a small degree of fraternal pride and then to deprecate it. "The place was very badly managed," said Stern.

Schindler dropped the envelope into Stern's lap. "This is their balance sheet. Tell me what you think."

Itzhak said that Herr Schindler should of course ask others as well as himself. Of course, Oskar told him. But I would value your opinion.

Stern read the balance sheets quickly; then, after some three minutes of study, all at once felt the strange silence of the office and looked up, finding Herr Oskar Schindler's eyes full on him.

There was, of course, in men like Stern an ancestral gift for sniffing out the just Goy, who could be used as buffer or partial refuge against the savageries of the others. It was a sense for where a safe house might be, a potential zone of shelter. And from now on the possibility of Herr Schindler as sanctuary would color the conversation. . . . It was a suggestion Stern was more aware of than Schindler, and nothing explicit would be said for fear of damaging the tender connection.

"It's a perfectly good business," said Stern. "You could speak to my brother. And, of course, now there's the possibility of military contracts. . . ."

"Exactly," murmured Herr Schindler.

For almost instantly after the fall of Cracow, even before Warsaw's siege ended, an Armaments Inspectorate had been set up in the Government General of Poland, its mandate being to enter into contracts with suitable manufacturers for the supply of army equipment. In a plant like Rekord, mess kits and field kitchenware could be turned out. The Armaments Inspectorate, Stern knew, was headed by a Major General Julius Schindler of the *Wehrmacht*. Was the general a relative of Herr Oskar Schindler's? Stern asked. No, I'm afraid not, said Schindler, but as if he wanted Stern to keep his nonrelationship a secret.

In any case, said Stern, even the skeleton production at Rekord was grossing more than a half-million złoty a year, and new metal-pressing plant and furnaces could be acquired relatively easily. It depended on Herr Schindler's access to credit.

Enamelware, said Schindler, was closer to his line than textiles. His background was in farm machinery, and he understood steam presses and so forth.

It did not any longer occur to Stern to ask why an elegant German entrepreneur wished to talk to him about business options. Meetings like this one had occurred throughout the history of his tribe, and the normal exchanges of business did not quite explain them. He talked on at some length, explaining how the Commercial Court would set the fee for the leasing of the bankrupt estate. Leasing with an option to buy—it was better than being a *Treuhänder*. As a *Treuhänder*, only a supervisor, you were completely under the control of the Economics Ministry.

Stern lowered his voice then and risked saying it: "You will find you are restricted in the people you'll be allowed to employ. . . ."

Schindler was amused. "How do you know all this? About ultimate intentions?"

"I read it in a copy of the *Berliner Tageblatt*. A Jew is still permitted to read German newspapers."

Schindler continued to laugh, reached out a hand, and let it fall on Stern's shoulder. "Is that so?" he asked.

In fact, Stern knew these things because Aue had received a directive from Reich Secretary of State Eberhard von Jagwitz of the Economics Ministry outlining the policies to be adopted in Aryanizing businesses. Aue had left it to Stern to make a digest of the memorandum. Von Jagwitz had indicated, more in sadness than in anger, that there would be pressure from other government and Party agencies, such as Heydrich's RHSA, the Reich Security Main Office, to Aryanize not just the ownership of companies, but also the management and work force. The sooner *Treuhänders* filtered out the skilled Jewish employees the better—always, of course, bearing in mind the maintenance of production at an acceptable level.

At last Herr Schindler put the accounts of Rekord back into his breast pocket, stood up, and led Itzhak Stern out into the main office. They stood there for a time, among the typists and clerks, growing philosophical, as Oskar liked to do. It was here that Oskar brought up the matter of Christianity's having its base in Judaism, a subject which for some reason, perhaps even because of his boyhood friendship with the Kantors in Zwittau, interested him. Stern spoke softly, at length, learnedly. He had published articles in journals of comparative religion. Oskar, who wrongly fancied himself a philosopher, had found an expert. The scholar himself, Stern, whom some thought a pedant, found Oskar's understanding shallow, a mind genial by nature but without much conceptual deftness. Not that Stern was about to complain. An ill-assorted friendship was firmly established. So that Stern found himself drawing an analogy, as Oskar's own father had, from previous empires and giving his own reasons why Adolf Hitler could not succeed.

The opinion slipped out before Stern could withdraw it. The other Jews in the office bowed their heads and stared fixedly at their worksheets. Schindler did not seem disturbed.

Near the end of their talk, Oskar did say something that had novelty. In times like these, he said, it must be hard for the churches to go on telling people that their Heavenly Father cared about the death of even a single sparrow. He'd hate to be a priest, Herr Schindler said, in an era like this, when life did not have the value of a pack of cigarettes. Stern agreed but suggested, in the spirit of the discussion, that the Biblical reference Herr Schindler had made could be summed up by a Talmudic verse which said that he who saves the life of one man saves the entire world.

"Of course, of course," said Oskar Schindler.

Itzhak, rightly or wrongly, always believed that it was at that moment that he had dropped the right seed in the furrow.

Schindler Comes Home

Richard Corliss

from *Time*, March 14, 1994

MEMORY is all we have, and when the memories are dreadful—when they hold images of the pain we have suffered or, perhaps even worse, inflicted—they are what we try to escape. The Nazi scheme to exterminate Jews and other undesirables is one such nightmare image; and *Schindler's List,* Steven Spielberg's drama about the man who saved 1,100 Jews from the Plaszow death camp, is essentially a plea by a preeminent popular artist that to remember is to speed the healing. Last week that moving Holocaust memorial became a mobile one, as the film opened in Germany, Poland and Israel—the three countries where the atrocities were planned, executed and most poignantly commemorated.

Thanks as much to its persuasive craftsmanship as to its wrenching theme, *Schindler's List* has already touched U.S. audiences. New Jersey Governor Christine Todd Whitman has arranged screenings as an intended antidote to hate crimes. But no audiences could feel a higher emotional stake in the subject than those last week at premieres in Frankfurt and other German cities, in Tel Aviv and Krakow. Viewers wept. Afterward many could not eat or sleep or talk. Some had been afraid to see it. Others said it should be seen by everyone. Spielberg, less a promoter for his film than a proselytizer for a spiritual unification of Germans and Jews, agreed. "I feel it is time in Germany for this generation to teach its children," he said. "Education is the way to stop another Holocaust from happening."

With President Richard von Weizsäcker in attendance, the film premiered in Frankfurt, the city where Schindler died in poverty in 1974. Then it moved to local theaters across the country. In Cologne's Cinedom, half a dozen young women collapsed sobbing in the arms of friends or parents. "I have never seen an audience behave like this," said Wolfgang Röhrig, a 26-year-old student. "It was as if they were in church. It was as if something sacred had happened."

What happened was the belated restoration of Oskar Schindler. In Israel, where he is buried, Schindler was a hero. In Poland, where he connived to save lives, he was a footnote in a history book. In Germany, where he was once sued for punching a man who called him a "Jew kisser," he was an embarrassment to all those who knew something and did nothing. And because amnesia is the most convenient placebo for collective guilt, Schindler was essentially a nonperson. In the '70s Artur Brauner, a German Jew, tried to make a movie about Schindler but could not raise the money. Now, with the release of Spielberg's film and several documentaries on the subject, Schindler has become a strange kind of celebrity, gnawing from beyond the grave at Germany's restless conscience.

If Germans were confronting their countrymen's bestiality in detail more vivid than some could stand, many Israelis were reluctant to relive it. "People here live the Holocaust," says Tel Aviv resident Noga Reshef, 29. "They teach it in school, they hold ceremonies, and every year there is Yom HaShoah, Holocaust Day. We can't escape the Holocaust; it sits on our shoulders." Others had more personal reasons for wanting to avoid the experience. "I'm afraid of these movies," said Pinchas Pistol, a Plaszow survivor who witnessed too much of the Nazis' random sadism. "Every time I see one, the memories come back, and I can't sleep or work." Yet he went, as did scores of other Holocaust survivors, as well as Prime Minister Yitzhak Rabin and President Ezer Weizman.

The official and popular response to *Schindler's List* was a mixture of benumbed awe and gratitude. But, as in the U.S., some critics charged that the film, by focusing on the few survivors of Nazi genocide rather than on the millions of dead, turned a continent's horror story into a fairy tale. In the Israeli daily *Ha'aretz*, historian Tom Segev dismissed it as "Spielberg's Holocaust Park," called the Auschwitz sequence "pornography" and concluded, "Spielberg needs the Holocaust, but the Holocaust does not need Spielberg." In the German newspaper *Die Welt*, critic Will Tremper headlined his review "Indiana Jones in the Krakow Ghetto." He excoriated Spielberg's vision as "pure Hollywood . . . the fantasies of a young boy from California who had never taken an interest in the Holocaust or the Jews before." Both critics were reflecting the view of Claude Lanzmann, director of the 1985 death-camp documentary *Shoah*. "It is seen from a very slanted angle, almost like an adventure story," Lanzmann wrote in London's *Evening Standard*. "Even if Spielberg believes that he has respected the historical truth, and I am sure he does, the general impression is distorting."

These antithetical, politically heretical opinions will only fuel interest in the film. In Vienna, 10,000 children quickly volunteered to see the 3-hour 15-minute movie. Yes, on a school day; but playing hooky will educate kids in the lesson of man's inhumanity to man—and of one man's humanity. To Michel Friedman, a child of *Schindlerjüden* and a leader in Frankfurt's Jewish community, Schindler's importance was not that he was a hero but that he was a human being: "a *Mensch*," says Friedman, using a good German and Yiddish word. "He is proof that if you wanted to help, even in 1944, even in Auschwitz, you could." And the response to *Schindler's List* is proof that the most offensive word in any language is *forget.*—*Reported by James O. Jackson/Bonn and Felice Marantz/Tel Aviv*

We Are Witnesses

Kenneth L. Woodward

from *Newsweek*, April 26, 1993

THE first thing that strikes you on entering the new United States Holocaust Memorial Museum, which President Bill Clinton is expected to dedicate this week, is how hard it is to see out from the inside. There's no clear view of the Washington Monument, the Jefferson Memorial or any of the buildings along the nearby mall that celebrate Freedom and Democracy, Enlightenment and Progress. That's how it should be. This is a history museum, and the story it tells forever shattered the Enlightenment illusion of human perfectibility. At every twisted turn, the museum's industrial architecture evokes the closed, monitored world of the Nazi death camps and the planned genocides in which 6 million Jews and 5 million others—Gypsies, Jehovah's Witnesses, . . . the handicapped, plus the entire Polish intelligentsia—were systematically exterminated in less than a decade. Dante is the poet of this space: "Abandon hope, all ye who enter here."

Controversial from the start, the museum dares speak memories that some camp survivors still regard as too sacred for words and images, too transcendently evil to be displayed in another time, another place. This is not the only Holocaust museum in the United States—another, smaller one opened this February in Los Angeles—but in design, scope and ambition it rivals Yad Vashem, Israel's memorial to the Nazis' victims. Inevitably, the building and its brutally explicit permanent exhibit raise many difficult questions. Why here rather than in Eastern Europe? Why now? Why memorialize *this* singular, Godforsaken episode in Jewish history when we still have no building recalling what the United States did to Native Americans or to its African slaves?

Those who have visited the camps in Europe, as I did 32 years ago, know the compelling need to remember what man has done—can do—to man. They will also recognize immediately the red brick façade of the first-floor Hall of Witness. The skylight above is a crosshatch of cold, contorted steel beams recalling the bleak testimony of the prisoners: the only thing the Nazis could not take from them was the daylight. To personalize the experience, each visitor is offered a computer-generated ID card with the picture of a Holocaust victim whose story can be followed by

145

inserting the card in monitors stationed throughout the exhibition. The doors of the elevators are gunmetal gray; they open and shut heavily, like the doors of an oven. But the initial sounds we hear inside are the shocked voices of American troops who liberated some of the camps in 1945. A plaque on the wall quotes Gen. Dwight D. Eisenhower's reaction to what he saw. This is another answer to why such a museum is necessary: despite the noxious arguments of revisionists who deny that the Holocaust took place, there *were* outside witnesses.

The entire exhibit, which works downward from the fourth floor and covers 36,000 square feet, requires at least three hours to experience and absorb. Along with posters, proclamations and other artifacts, two brief films document the rise of German anti-Semitism and Adolf Hitler's creation of a police state. Jews are tagged and numbered, ghettoized as non-Aryans, deprived of civil rights. Kristallnacht (Nov. 9, 1938) is memorialized with charred Torahs and scenes of plundered Jewish shops.

Not surprisingly, the German government has objected to this reconstruction of its Nazi past and has asked that the museum create an additional exhibit on postwar German democracy—a request the museum's directors vigorously rejected. But, as the permanent exhibition makes clear, there is enough guilt for several countries to share. Ample space is devoted to the Evian Conference, called by President Franklin D. Roosevelt in 1938, at which representatives of a dozen nations turned their backs on Jews trying to escape the Third Reich. Here, too, is the story of the St. Louis, the shipload of Jewish emigrants who were refused asylum in the United States and returned to their Nazi tormentors. What did Americans know of the Holocaust and when did they know it? Front-page newspaper reports show that readers in New York, St. Louis and other cities were informed of Hitler's genocide plans as early as 1933. "This is one of the important reasons for the museum," says Raye Farr, a filmmaker who is director of the permanent exhibition. "The role of the bystander is central to the story we have to tell."

On the third floor the story lunges dizzyingly from purgatory to hell. A cobblestone street and a wooden bridge introduce visitors to the Warsaw ghetto, created in 1933 to isolate and eventually eliminate a half-million Jews. There's a milk can, one of two in which historian Emanuel Ringelblum buried his archive of ghetto life. A film shows Nazis trucking off aged hospital patients to their deaths. Here's the gate of the Jewish cemetery in Tarnow, Poland, where hundreds of Jews were rounded up and shot. Other exhibits depict the mobile death squads that followed German troops into the Soviet Union and wiped out entire villages in an afternoon. A cattle car like those used to transport Jews to the camps stands at a mock siding, open for boarding. On the other side, we observe pictures of stunned Jews, husbands separated from wives and children. To the side are mounds of eyeglasses, combs, toothbrushes and suitcases. Overhead is a cast of the mocking entry sign to Auschwitz: ARBEIT MACHT FREI (WORK WILL MAKE YOU FREE).

Then come the voices, and we take a needed pause to sit and listen to transcriptions of survivors telling their tales. We enter a reassembled barracks from Birkenau that includes the hard wooden bunks where emaciated prisoners slept six in a space fit for two. Here, too, are the striped uniforms, the food bowls and crude shoes which were all that prisoners could call their own. Altogether, the museum has collected 23,000 of these nightmare artifacts. And then, there it is: the cast of a gas chamber plus several canisters of Zyklon B—fumes of the Final Solution.

Mass graves: But there is more—maybe too much more. Across a glass bridge we enter the final destination. On one side, a heap of 4,000 shoes. On another, a mural of bald female inmates, blank-eyed in their humiliation. The museum was prepared to display bales of hair, which the Germans used to stuff their pillows, but survivors on the museum committee wouldn't permit it. "That could be my mother's hair," one member objected. In an adjacent alcove is an oven, beside it the zinc-lined table where teeth were relieved of gold fillings. At last we enter a square, three-story tower. Covering the walls are 1,500 photographs reflecting the entire population of Ejszyszki, a once lively *shtetl* (village) in rural southern Poland. All but 29 survivors were machine-gunned and dumped into mass graves.

The museum strains to end on an upbeat note. It harbors a wooden boat of the kind the Danes used to ferry Jews to Sweden. There's a tribute to Raoul Wallenberg and other "righteous Gentiles" who risked their lives to hide and save Jews. The one noticeable omission is the thousands of Christian clergy, Protestant and Roman Catholic, who were also interned and liquidated in the camps. Fittingly, the museum's domed, hexagonal Hall of Remembrance allows visitors to sit and meditate on the horror of it all, in the glow of an eternal flame. Silence is needed to assimilate what happened—and to realize that mass extermination is a recurring nightmare. It is happening again in parts of Africa and, especially now, in the former Yugoslavia. Another reason to remember.

The museum also hopes to educate. Its archives are open to scholars; although museum officials caution against letting children under 11 view the permanent exhibit, they offer outreach programs for schools and churches. But there are limits to turning the Holocaust into an educational experience. In L.A., for instance, the Simon Wiesenthal Center's Museum of Tolerance provides a similar re-creation of the Holocaust. Designed for what director Dr. Gerald Margolis calls "the intelligent 17-year-old," it displays a sequence of miniature scenes and videos dramatizing how Hitler achieved power in a democracy and then executed a plan to exterminate Europe's Jews. The hourlong exhibition concludes with videos of the camps that visitors watch while sitting in a darkened concrete room which strongly resembles a gas chamber.

So far, the museum has been a success, drawing an average of 1,000 visitors a day. But in their efforts to attract the public, museum officials have handicapped their presentation with a didactic opening exhibition aimed at exposing hidden prejudices and behavior in American life. Visitors must first pass through a neon-lit interactive game room in which they are taught to recognize—and reject—racist, sexist and other stereotypes. A half hour of this soft-core political correctness and you yearn for a monologue from Don Rickles. Valuable though these preliminary lessons in civility may be—particularly for tense, multicultural L.A.—they do not prepare visitors for encountering the Holocaust.

Indeed, although the Holocaust occurred on foreign soil, the decision to memorialize its victims on the Washington Mall seems right, if not altogether just. "The building is a seal that the Holocaust happened," says Edward Linenthal, a professor of religious studies at the University of Wisconsin in Oshkosh who is writing a book on the museum's history. "It's also an insurance policy that Jews are welcome in America." But monuments can bind as well as release memory. The Holocaust Museum will succeed if, like its eternal flame, it continues to shed light on surpassing darkness.

from
The Sunflower

Simon Wiesenthal

Simon Wiesenthal was a prisoner in a Nazi death camp during World War II. One day a nurse brought him into the presence of a young, dying man whose head was wrapped in bandages. The man was a Nazi, a member of the dreaded SS. Slowly, in great physical and emotional pain, he told Wiesenthal his life story—that he was raised to be religious, how he joined the Hitler Youth, and later the SS, how his father became distant because of this, although his mother remained constant and loving. Hours later, the soldier finally confessed to a terrible crime—forcing hundreds of Jews into a building, setting the building on fire, and shooting any Jew who tried to escape the flames.

The Nazi struggled to a sitting position, and clasped his hands together as if for prayer. He begged forgiveness for his crimes, saying that without an answer he could not die in peace. Wiesenthal stared at the pitiable figure, then left without saying a word.

The memory of that day haunted Wiesenthal for years to come. He wondered if he had made the right choice—withholding forgiveness and denying comfort to a dying man who was obviously repentant. Finally, his guilt forced him to seek out the man's parents in hopes of finding some sort of answer.

I CLIMBED the decrepit, dusty stairs and knocked on the shattered wooden door. There was no immediate response and I prepared myself for the disappointment of an unfulfilled mission. Suddenly the door opened gratingly, and a small, frail old lady appeared on the threshold.

"Are you Frau Maria S——?" I asked.

"Yes," she answered.

"May I speak to you and your husband?"

"I am a widow."

She bade me come in and I looked around the room, the walls of which were cracked and the plaster on the ceiling was loose. Over the sideboard hung, not quite straight, a photograph of a good-looking, bright-eyed boy. Around one corner of the picture there was a black band. I had no doubt this was the photograph of the man who had sought my forgiveness. He was an only son. I went over to the photo and looked at the eyes that I had never seen.

"That is my son, Karl," said the woman in a broken voice. "He was killed in the war."

"I know," I murmured.

I had not yet told her why I had come, indeed I had not yet made up my mind what I wanted to say. On the way to Stuttgart many thoughts had run through my head. Originally I had wanted to talk to the mother to check the truth of the story he had told me. But was I not secretly hoping that I might hear something that contradicted it? It would certainly make things easier for me. The feeling of sympathy which I could not reject would then perhaps disappear. I reproached myself for not having planned to open the conversation. Now that I confronted the mother I did not know how to begin.

I stood in front of Karl's portrait in silence: I could not take my eyes off him. His mother noticed it. "He was my only son, a dear good boy. So many young men of his age are dead. What can one do? There is so much pain and suffering today, and I am left all alone."

Many other mothers had also been left all alone, I thought. She invited me to sit down. I looked at her grief-stricken face and said: "I am bringing you greetings from your son."

"Is this really true? Did you know him? It is almost four years since he died. I got the news from the hospital. They sent his things back to me."

She stood up and opened an old chest from which she took the very same bundle the hospital nurse had tried to give me.

"I have kept his things here, his watch, his notebook and a few other trifles . . . Tell me, when did you see him?"

I hesitated. I did not want to destroy the woman's memory of her "good" son.

"Four years ago I was working on the Eastern Railway at Lemberg," I began. "One day, while we were working there, a hospital train drew up bringing wounded from the east. We talked to some of them through the windows. One of them handed me a note with your address on it and asked me to convey to you greetings from one of his comrades, if ever I had the opportunity to do so."

I was rather pleased with this quick improvisation.

"So actually you never saw him?" she asked.

"No," I answered. "He was probably so badly wounded that he could not come to the window."

"How then was he able to write?" she questioned. "His eyes were injured, and all the letters he sent to me must have been dictated to one of the nurses."

"Perhaps he had asked one of his comrades to write down your address," I said hesitatingly.

"Yes," she reflected, "it must have been like that. My son was so devoted to me. He was not on specially good terms with his father, although he too loved our son as much as I did."

She broke off for a moment and looked around the room.

"Forgive me, please, for not offering you anything," she apologised, "I should very much like to do so, but you know how things are today. I have nothing in the house and there is very little in the shops."

I stood up and went over to her son's photograph again. I did not know how to bring the conversation round again to him.

"Take the photograph down if you like," she suggested. I took it carefully down from the wall and put it on the table.

"Is that a uniform he is wearing?" I asked.

"Yes, he was sixteen at the time and in the Hitler Youth," she replied. "My husband did not like it at all: he was a convinced Social Democrat, and he had many difficulties because he would not join the Party. Now I am glad he didn't. In all those years he never got any promotion; he was always passed over. It was only during the war that he was at last made manager, because all the younger men were called up. Only a few weeks later, almost exactly a year from the day on which we received news of our son's death, the factory was bombed. Many lost their lives—including my husband."

In a helpless, despairing gesture she folded her hands together.

"So I am left all alone. I live only for the memories of my husband and my son. I might move to my sister's, but I don't want to give up this house. My parents lived here and my son was born here. Everything reminds me of the happy times, and if I went away I feel I should be denying the past."

As my eyes came to rest on a crucifix which hung on the wall, the old lady noticed my glance.

"I found that cross in the ruins of a house. It was buried in the rubble, except that one arm was showing, pointing up accusingly to the sky. As nobody seemed to want it I took it away. I feel a little less abandoned."

Had this woman too perhaps thought God was on leave and had returned to the world only when he saw all the ruins? Before I could pursue this train of thought, she went on: "What happened to us was a punishment from God. My husband said at the time of Hitler's coming to power that it would end in disaster. Those were prophetic words: I am always thinking about them . . .

"One day our boy surprised us with the news that he had joined the Hitler Youth, although I had brought him up on strictly religious lines. You may have noticed the saints' pictures in the room. Most of them I had to take down after 1933—my son asked me to do so. His comrades used to rag him for being crazy about the Church. He told me about it reproachfully as if it were my fault. You know how in those days they set our children against God and their parents. My husband was not a very religious man. He rarely went to church because he did not like the priests, but he would allow nothing to be said against our parish priest, for Karl was his favorite. It always made my husband happy to hear the priest's praise . . ."

The old lady's eyes filled with tears. She took the photograph in her hand and gazed at it. Her tears fell on the glass . . .

I once saw in a gallery an old painting of a mother holding a picture of her missing son. Here, it had come to life.

"Ah," she sighed, "if you only knew what a fine young fellow our son was. He was always ready to help without being asked. At school he was really a model pupil—till he joined the Hitler Youth, and that completely altered him. From then on he refused to go to church."

She was silent for a while as she recalled the past. "The result was a sort of split in the family. My husband did not talk much, as was his habit, but I could feel how upset he was. For instance, if he wanted to talk about somebody who had been arrested by the Gestapo, he first looked round to be sure that his own son was not listening . . . I stood helplessly between my man and my child."

Again she sank into a reverie. "Then the war began and my son came home with the news that he had volunteered. For the SS; of course. My husband was horrified. He did not reproach Karl—but he practically stopped talking to him . . . right up to the day of his departure. Karl went to war without a single word from his father.

"During his training he sent us snapshots but my husband always pushed the photos aside. He did not want to look at his son in SS uniform. Once I told him, 'We have to live with Hitler, like millions of others. You know what the neighbors think of us. You will have difficulties at the factory.'

"He only answered: 'I simply can't pretend. They have even taken our son away from us.' He said the same thing when Karl left us. He seemed to have written Karl off as his son."

I listened intently to the woman and I nodded occasionally, to encourage her to continue. She could not tell me enough.

I had previously talked to many Germans and Austrians, and learned from them how National Socialism had affected them. Most said they had been against it, but were frightened of their neighbors. And their neighbors had likewise been frightened of them. When one added together all these fears, the result was a frightful accumulation of mistrust.

There were many people like Karl's parents, but what about the people who did not need to knuckle under, because they had readily accepted the new regime? National Socialism was for them the fulfilment of their dearest wishes. It lifted them out of their insignificance. That it should come to power at the expense of innocent victims did not worry them. They were in the winners' camp and they severed relations with the losers. They expressed the contempt of the strong for the weak, the superman's scorn for the sub-human.

I looked at the old lady who was clearly kind-hearted, a good mother and a good wife. Without doubt she must often have shown sympathy for the oppressed, but the happiness of her own family was of paramount importance to her. There were millions of such families anxious only for peace and quiet in their own little nests. These were the mounting blocks by which the criminals climbed to power and kept it.

Should I now tell the old lady the naked truth? Should I tell her what her "good" boy had done in the name of his leaders?

What link was there between me, who might have been among her son's victims, and her, a lonely woman grieving for the ruin of her family amid the ruins of her people?

I saw her grief and I knew my own grief. Was sorrow our common link? Was it possible for grief to be an affinity?

I did not know the answers to these questionings.

Suddenly the woman resumed her recollections.

"One day they fetched the Jews away. Among them was our family doctor. According to the propaganda, the Jews were to be re-settled. It was said that Hitler was giving them a whole province in which they could live undisturbed among their own people. But later I heard of the brutality with which the SS treated them. My son was in Poland at the time and people talked of the awful things that were happening there. One day my husband said: 'Karl is with the SS over there. Perhaps the positions are reversed and he is now treating our doctor, who formerly treated him—'

"My husband would not say what he meant by that. But I knew he was upset. I was very depressed."

Suddenly the old lady looked at me intently.

"You are not a German?" she ventured.

"No," I replied, "I am a Jew."

She became a little embarrassed. At that time all Germans were embarrassed when they met Jews.

She hastened to tell me:

"In this district we always lived with the Jews in a very peaceful fashion. We are not responsible for their fate."

"Yes," said I, "that is what they all say now. And I can well believe it of you, but there are others from whom I won't take it. The question of Germany's guilt may never be settled. But one thing is certain: no German can shrug off the responsibility. Even if he has no personal guilt, he must share the shame of it. As a member of a guilty nation he cannot simply walk away like a passenger leaving a tramcar, whenever he chooses. It is the duty of Germans to find out who was guilty. And the non-guilty must dissociate themselves publicly from the guilty."

I felt I had spoken sharply. The lonely widow looked at me sadly. She was not the person with whom one could debate about the sins and the guilt of the Germans.

This broken woman, so deeply immersed in grief, was no recipient for my reproaches. I was sorry for her. Perhaps I should not have raised the issue of guilt.

"I can't really believe the stories that they tell," she went on. "I can't believe what they say happened to the Jews. During the war there were so many different stories. My husband was the only person who seemed to have known the truth. Some of his workmen had been out east setting up machinery, and when they came back they told of things even my husband would not believe, although he knew that the Party was capable of anything. He did not tell me much of what he had heard. Probably he was afraid I might gossip unthinkingly, and then we get into trouble with the Gestapo, who were already ill-disposed towards us and kept a watchful eye on my husband. But as our Karl was with the SS they did not molest us. Some of our friends and acquaintances got into trouble—they had been denounced by their best friends.

"My husband told me once that a Gestapo official had been to see him at the works, where foreigners were employed. He was inquiring into a case of sabotage. He talked to my husband for a long time, and finally said, 'You are above suspicion, for your son is with the SS.'

"When Father came home and told me what had happened, he said bitterly: 'They have turned the world upside down. The one thing that has hurt me more than anything else in my life is now my protection.' He simply could not understand it."

I gazed at the lonely woman sitting sadly with her memories. I formed a picture of how she lived. I knew that from time to time she would take in her arms her son's bundle, his last present, as if it were her son himself.

"I can well believe what people said—so many dreadful things happened. But one thing is certain, Karl never did any wrong. He was always a decent young man. I miss him so much now that my husband is dead. . ." I thought of the many mothers who were also bereft of their sons.

But her son had not lied to me; his home was just as he had described it. Yet the solution of my problem was not a single step nearer . . .

I took my leave without diminishing in any way the poor woman's last surviving consolation—faith in the goodness of her son.

Perhaps it was a mistake not to have told her the truth. Perhaps her tears might help to wash away some of the misery of the world.

That was not the only thought that occurred to me. I knew there was little I could say to this mother, and whatever I might have told her about her son's crime she would not have believed.

She would prefer to think me a slanderer than acknowledge Karl's crime.

She kept repeating the words: "He was such a good boy," as if she wished me to confirm it. But that I could not do. Would she still have the same opinion of him if she knew all?

In his boyhood Karl had certainly been a "good boy." But a graceless period of his life had turned him into a murderer.

My picture of Karl was almost complete. His physical likeness too was now established, for in his mother's home I had at last seen his face.

I knew all about his childhood and I knew all about the crime he had committed. And was pleased with myself for not having told his mother of his wicked deed. I convinced myself that I had acted rightly. In her present circumstances, to take from her her last possession would probably have also been a crime.

Today, I sometimes think of the young SS man. Every time I enter a hospital, every time I see a nurse, or a man with his head bandaged, I recall him.

Or when I see a sunflower . . .

And I reflect that people like him are still being born; people who can be indoctrinated with evil. Mankind is ostensibly striving to avert catastrophes; medical progress gives us hope that one day disease can be conquered, but will we ever be able to prevent the creation of mass murderers?

The work in which I am engaged brings me into contact with many known murderers. I hunt them out, I hear witnesses, I give evidence in courts—and I see how murderers behave when accused.

At the trial of Nazis in Stuttgart only one of the accused showed remorse. He actually confessed to deeds to which there were no witnesses. All the others bitterly disputed the truth. Many of them regretted only one thing—that witnesses had survived to tell the truth.

I have often tried to imagine how that young SS man would have behaved if he had been put on trial twenty-five years later.

Would he have spoken in court as he did to me before he died in the Dean's room? Would he openly admit what he had confessed to me on his deathbed?

Perhaps the picture that I had formed of him in my mind was kinder than the reality. I never saw him in the camp with a whip in his hand, I saw him only on his deathbed—a man who wanted absolution for his crime.

Was he thus an exception?

I could find no answer to that question. How could I know if he would have committed further crimes had he survived?

I have a fairly detailed knowledge of the life story of many Nazi murderers. Few of them were born murderers. They had mostly been peasants, manual laborers, clerks or officials, such as one meets in normal everyday life. In their youth they had received religious instruction; and none had a previous criminal record. Yet they became murderers; expert murderers by conviction. It was as if they had taken down their SS uniforms from the wardrobe and replaced them with their consciences as well as with their civilian clothes.

I couldn't possibly know their reactions to their first crimes, but I do know that every one of them had subsequently murdered on a wholesale scale.

When I recall the insolent replies and the mocking grins of many of these accused, it is difficult for me to believe that my repentant young SS man would also have behaved in that way . . . Yet ought I to have forgiven him? Today the world demands that we forgive and forget the heinous crimes committed against us. It urges that we draw a line, and close the account as if nothing had ever happened.

We who suffered in those dreadful days, we who cannot obliterate the hell we endured, are forever being advised to keep silent.

Well, I kept silent when a young Nazi, on his deathbed, begged me to be his confessor. And later when I met his mother I again kept silent rather than shatter her illusions about her dead son's inherent goodness. And how many bystanders kept silent as they watched Jewish men, women, and children being led to the slaughterhouses of Europe?

There are many kinds of silence. Indeed it can be more eloquent than words, and it can be interpreted in many ways.

Was my silence at the bedside of the dying Nazi right or wrong? This is a profound moral question that challenges the conscience of the reader of this episode, just as much as it once challenged my heart and my mind. There are those who can appreciate my dilemma, and so endorse my attitude, and there are others who will be ready to condemn me for refusing to ease the last moments of a repentant murderer.

The crux of the matter is, of course, the question of forgiveness. Forgetting is something that time alone takes care of, but forgiveness is an act of volition, and only the sufferer is qualified to make the decision.

You, who have just read this sad and tragic episode in my life, can mentally change places with me and ask yourself the crucial question, "What would I have done?"

Acknowledgments *(continued from p. ii)*

W. W. Norton & Company
Introduction to "Holocaust Witness Elie Wiesel . . ." by William Safire, from *Lend Me Your Ears: Great Speeches in History*, Revised Edition by William Safire, editor. Copyright © 1992, 1997 by The Cobbett Corporation. Reprinted by permission of W. W. Norton & Company, Inc.

Schocken Books, a Division of Random House, Inc., and Vallentine, Mitchell & Company Ltd.
"We gathered flowers . . . ," "You are not alone . . . ," and Blessed is the Match . . . " from *Hannah Senesh: Her Life and Diary* by Hannah Senesh, translated by Marta Cohn. Copyright © 1971 by Nigel Marsh. Reprinted by permission of Schocken Books, distributed by Pantheon Books, a division of Random House, Inc., and Vallentine, Mitchell & Company Ltd.

Time Life Syndication
"Schindler Comes Home" by Richard Corliss from *Time Magazine* March 14, 1994. Copyright 1994 Time Life Syndication. Used by permission of Time Life Syndication.

Touchstone Books, a division of Simon & Schuster
From *Schindler's List* by Thomas Keneally. Copyright © 1982 by Serpentine Publishing Co. Pty Ltd.

Viking Penguin, a division of Penguin Putnam Inc.
From *If This Is a Man (Survival in Auschwitz)* by Primo Levi, translated by Stuart Woolf. Translation copyright © 1959 by Orion Press, Inc., © 1958 by Giulio Einaudi editore S.P.A. Used by permission of Viking Penguin, a division of Penguin Putnam Inc.

Watkins Loomis Agency for John Bierman
From *Righteous Gentile* by John Bierman. Copyright © 1981 by John Bierman. "A Jewish Cemetery Near Leningrad" by Josef Brodsky and excerpt from "To My Friends" by N. Nor, from *Russia's Underground Poets* selected and translated by Keith Bosley with Dimitry Pospielovsky and Janis Sapiets. © 1968 Possev-Verlag, V. Gorachek KG. English translation © 1968 Keith Bosley, Dimitry Pospielovsky.

Weidenfeld & Nicolson, a subsidiary of Orion Publishing Group Ltd.
From *Simon Wiesenthal: A Life in Search of Justice* by Hella Pick. Copyright 1996 by Hella Pick. Reprinted by permission of Weidenfeld & Nicolson, an imprint of The Orion Publishing Group Ltd.

Zephyr Press
"All the Unburied Ones" from *The Complete Poems of Anna Akhmatova*, Volume II, translated by Judith Hemschemeyer, edited by Roberta Reeder. Translation copyright © 1989, 1992, 1997 by Judith Hemschemeyer. Reprinted by permission of Zephyr Press.

Note: Every effort has been made to locate the copyright owner of material reprinted in this book. Omissions brought to our attention will be corrected in subsequent editions.